Y0-EMC-432

Arizona's All-Time Baseball Team
Published by John J. Rust at Createspace
Copyright © 2015 John J. Rust

The author has made every attempt to make certain the information contained in this book is accurate. Multiple sources were used in the research of this book. Many of those sources are cited within the body. The author and publisher assume no responsibility for errors or omissions. The author and publisher assume no liability for any damages resulting from the use of information contained within this book. The players named in the simulated games in this book are used in a fictitious manner.

Stats, league leaders and rosters presented within this book were obtained from baseball-reference.com. Other reference material came from *The Arizona Republic, The Arizona Daily Star,* The Arizona Interscholastic Association, the Arizona Sports Hall of Fame, the Mesa City Hall of Fame, the Prescott High School Hall of Fame, the Pima County Hall of Fame and various college and university athletic websites.

ACKNOWLEDGMENTS

There are many people to thank for making this book a reality. Ted Blake, Pat Brock, Kelly Cordes, Mike Cornish, Jerry Dawson, Les Fenderson, Michael Hanson, Jerry Kindall, Rod Soesbe and Kent Winslow for taking time out to be interviewed about the players and coaches featured in this book. Another thank you goes to the sports information departments at Arizona State University and the University of Arizona, as well as the Arizona Historical Society, for providing me with contact information for the people interviewed for this book and for fact checking some of the details presented in this book. Finally, thank you to my parents for their continued love and support.

Other Books by John J. Rust

Dark Wings

Sea Raptor

The Best Phillies Team Ever

PROLOGUE

Arizona. There's more to it than the Old West and enormous holes in the ground. The state is also famous for another reason.

Producing a lot of good baseball players.

According to Prescott's Sharlot Hall Museum, the first recorded baseball game in the Arizona Territory took place in 1873. The *Arizona Miner* newspaper reported the contest was held on a January afternoon between two unnamed teams that ended with an unknown result. More games took place over the next few decades, leading to the University of Arizona fielding its very first baseball team in 1904, eight years before statehood. They ended up with a 6-1 record in their first season. Not to be outdone, UofA's rival, the Tempe Normal School – known today as Arizona State University – put together its own team in 1907. Professional baseball debuted in Arizona in 1915 with the formation of the Class D Rio Grande Association, with three of the six teams residing in the newly minted state; the Douglas Miners, the Tucson Old Pueblos and the Phoenix Senators. Unfortunately, the league folded after just one year.

In 1928, the pros returned to the Grant Canyon State with the formation of the Arizona State League. With teams like the Bisbee Bees, Tucson Cowboys, Mesa Jewels, Globe Bears and, once again, the Phoenix Senators, this league fared better than the Rio Grande Association. It lasted three seasons instead of one.

In 1931, the Arizona State League gave way to the Arizona-Texas League, which played on and off until 1954.

The state also hosted spring training in 1929, but only for one game when the Detroit Tigers took on the Pittsburgh Pirates on March 26th. Eighteen years passed before another spring training game took place in the desert. But that year, 1947, would ultimately cement Arizona's reputation as a baseball state. That was the year the Cactus League was born.

Not that it started out as much of a league. In that first year, only two teams held spring training in Arizona, the New York Giants and the Cleveland Indians. From that very humble beginning, the Cactus League has gotten bigger. Much bigger. Fifteen MLB teams now make their spring training homes in the greater Phoenix area.

The end of spring training, however, did not mean the end of professional baseball in Arizona. In 1958, when the major leaguers left the desert, fans could sit out in sweltering, triple-digit temperatures and watch their new AAA ball club, the Phoenix Giants. With future major league stars like Willie McCovey and Felipe Alou, the Giants won the Pacific Coast League Championship in their inaugural season. They followed that up with a dismal 64-90 record in 1959. That was followed by the team moving to Washington State to become the Tacoma Giants in 1960.

Arizona wasn't without minor league baseball for long. In 1966, the Giants abandoned Tacoma and returned to Phoenix. Three years later, Southern Arizona got its own minor league team as the Chicago White Sox put their AAA affiliate in Tucson. The Toros, renamed the Sidewinders in 1998, played there for nearly 40 years before the franchise moved to Reno, Nevada. Replacing them in 2011 were the Tucson Padres, who stayed for three seasons before relocating to El Paso, Texas.

The Phoenix Giants, meanwhile, changed their name to the Phoenix Firebirds in 1986. They remained in the Valley of the Sun until 1997, when they moved to Fresno, California to make way for Arizona's long-awaited entry into Major League Baseball. In 1998, the expansion Arizona Diamondbacks took the field for the first time at Bank One Ballpark – later Chase Field – a retractable roof stadium, meaning fans did not have to swelter in desert heat as they did at Phoenix Municipal Stadium and Scottsdale Stadium watching the Giants and Firebirds.

Arizona's ball clubs experienced much success over the decades. Luis Gonzalez capped off an incredible ninth inning comeback against the vaunted New York Yankees with a walk-off single to give the D-backs the 2001 World Championship. They also picked up NL West Division titles in 1999, 2002, 2007 and 2011. The Phoenix Giants won their second PCL title in 1977, while the Tucson Toros were PCL champs in 1991 and 1993, then won another championship in 2006 as the Sidewinders. In the collegiate ranks, ASU captured five National Championships (1965, 1967, 1969, 1977 and 1981), while UofA took home college baseball's grand prize four times (1976, 1980, 1986 and 2012). Grand Canyon University won four NAIA World Series titles (1980, 1981, 1982 and 1986). The state's junior colleges have also built winning traditions, with national championships won by Yavapai College (1975, 1977 and 1993), Phoenix College (1960, 1962 and 1965), Mesa College (1970, 1971 and 1972), Central Arizona College (1976 and 2002) and Glendale College (1968). These and other Arizona colleges have sent over 300 players to the Majors. Some of the names you might recognize. Dustin Pedroia, Reggie Jackson, Barry Bonds, Trevor Hoffman, Kenny Lofton, Hubie Brooks and Bengie Molina.

But I will not be dealing with players who came from other states and countries to suit up for Arizona's various professional and college teams. The 25-man roster featured in this book is made up of players either born in Arizona or who were raised in the state and at least graduated from high school. Ninety-five Major League players were born in Arizona, with several transplants spending the majority of their youth in the state. Of all those players, who is good enough to make the starting line up, the starting rotation, the bullpen and the bench of Arizona's All-Time Baseball Team?

We're about to find out.

FIRST BASE

The first player on this roster is someone who didn't start out as an Arizona resident. He also didn't start out as a first baseman. His family moved from New England to Scottsdale, and he spent much of his high school career as a catcher.

His name is Paul Konerko.

Born in Providence, Rhode Island, Konerko's family relocated to Arizona when he was eleven. A few years later, he became part of the Chaparral High School baseball program, and didn't have to wait long to crack the varsity roster. Konerko was called up late in his freshman season. From that point on, he re-wrote the Firebird record book.

In a three-and-a-half year varsity career, Konerko set single season records in batting average (.558) and doubles (18). Both marks stood for over a decade until they were surpassed by current Oakland A's first baseman Ike Davis. Konerko also had the most career doubles in Chaparral history until, once again, Davis broke that record. For home runs and RBIs, Konerko is still number one in those categories all-time, with 21 and 132 respectively. His coach at Chaparral, Jerry Dawson, said, "He was an outstanding hitter. In my 37 years as a high school coach, he is, by far, the best high school hitter I've ever seen. Just a pure hitter. He could roll out of bed and hit."

In 1994, Konerko's abilities at the plate and behind it helped Chaparral capture its first state championship. He had such an impressive senior season he was named the *Arizona Republic/Phoenix Gazette* Player of the Year and was ranked the number one catcher in the nation. Dawson said, "He was an outstanding defensive catcher, who threw the ball extremely well, and was very accurate. He was very agile behind the plate for a big man. He was very cerebral, which helped him be a good catcher."

All those stats and accolades impressed the Los Angeles Dodgers so much they drafted Konerko in the first round and assigned him to their

Single-A short season team, the Yakima Bears. He had no problem jumping from high school right to the pros. In 67 games, Konerko hit .288 with six home runs, 58 RBIs and 15 doubles.

The farther up the minor league ladder he climbed, the better he got. Splitting his time between AA San Antonio and AAA Albuquerque in 1996, Konerko hit .304 with 30 homers, 88 RBIs, 23 doubles and 80 runs scored.

Because of hip problems stemming in part from his years playing youth hockey, the Dodgers made him switch positions from catcher to first base. Dawson recalled the story Konerko and his father told him of the day the Dodgers informed them of the change.

"They had breakfast with the Dodgers GM, and when they walked into breakfast, the GM laid a first baseman's mitt on the table in front of them and said, 'Here's your new glove. Learn how to play it.'"

Konerko did learn to play his new position, and play it very well. He committed 14 errors in 1,250 chances in 1996 and ended up with a .989 fielding percentage. Dawson said, "He worked hard on his defense. He was out at the high school field every day, taking ground balls at first. He sought out people in the Dodgers organization, ex-players and former first basemen that he knew. He was honing his craft. He had to learn a new position, and if he was going to learn it, he was going to learn it well. "

The next season, Konerko tore up the Pacific Coast League, hitting at a .323 clip with 37 homers, 127 RBIs, 31 doubles and 97 runs scored. Those numbers earned him three things. The first was the league MVP, the second was *Baseball America's* 1997 Minor League Player of the Year award.

The third was a September call up.

Konerko made his Major League debut on September 8th, 1997, little over three years after graduating from Chaparral. He played in just six games for the Dodgers with only one hit in seven at-bats.

In 1998, Konerko not only split his time between the majors and the minors, but between different franchises. On the day America celebrated its 222nd birthday – that would be July 4th – Konerko and pitcher Dennys Reyes were traded to the Cincinnati Reds for Jeff Shaw, who led the National League in saves the year before with 42. In 75 games between the Dodgers and Reds, Konerko hit .217 with seven home runs and 29 RBIs. Convinced they could do better, the powers that be in Cincy traded him to the Chicago White Sox for Mike Cameron.

Now the pressure was really on the former Firebird. With Frank Thomas being used more and more as a designated hitter, The Palehose needed another power hitting first baseman.

Konerko stepped up to the plate, figuratively and literally. In his first year in Chicago, he batted .294 with 24 homers, 81 RBIs, 31 doubles and 71 runs scored. His stats only got better from there. In 2000, Konerko upped his average and RBI total to .298 and 97 respectively, while hitting 21 home runs, 31 doubles and scoring 84 runs. In the field, he made just ten errors at first and wound up with a fielding percentage of .991. It all helped the White Sox win the American League Central Division title. Unfortunately for Konerko, his offense abandoned him in the Divisional Series. He went 0-10 at the plate with one walk as Chicago was swept in three games by the Seattle Mariners.

Konerko came back with a vengeance in 2001. He hit .282 with 32 home runs, 99 RBIs, 35 doubles, 92 runs scored and a .507 slugging percentage. 2002 would be just as good as he hit .304 with 27 homers, 104 RBIs, 30 doubles and 81 runs scored, and earned his first of six American League All-Star selections. In addition, Konerko was named the AL's Player of the Month for June.

After posting career highs in home runs and RBIs with 41 and 117 in 2004, Konerko had another big season in 2005. He clubbed 40 round-trippers while batting .283 with 100 RBIs, 24 doubles and a single-season best 98 runs scored. Along with his second All-Star selection, he also made his second trip to the post-season.

This time, he did not disappoint.

In the Divisional Series vs. Boston, he hit .250 with two homers, four RBIs and three runs scored. One of those dingers was a go-ahead two-run bomb off Tim Wakefield to break a 2-2 tie in Game Three. The White Sox ultimately won 5-3 to sweep the Red Sox.

Next came AL Championship Series vs. the Los Angeles Angels of Anaheim, California. After being relatively quiet in the first two games, Konerko woke up.

Boy did he wake up.

In the first inning of Game Three, Konerko took John Lackey deep for a two-run shot. He struck again in the fifth with an RBI single as Chicago defeated LA 5-2. In Game Four, Konerko homered again, this time plating three runs as the Chisox overpowered the Angels 8-2. He also had an RBI double in Game Five as the White Sox triumphed 6-3 to win the AL pennant and head to the World Series for the first time since 1959.

When all was said and done, Konerko batted .286 in five games with two homers and seven RBIs and was named the MVP of the AL Championship Series.

In the Fall Classic, the Chaparral alum had his big moment in the seventh inning of Game Two when he blasted a grand slam off Houston's Chad Qualls. The White Sox swept the Astros in four games to win their first World Championship since 1917.

Along with being a great slugger, Konerko was also a great clubhouse leader. The White Sox named him their team captain in 2006. After the firing of manager Ozzie Guillen in 2011, General Manager Kenny Williams actually considered naming Konerko player-manager. That, of course, never materialized, and the Sox went with former third baseman Robin Ventura as their new skipper.

Konerko continued putting up big numbers into the early 2010s, with 111 RBIs in 2010 and 105 in 2011, giving him six seasons of 100-plus runs driven in. He also socked 39 and 31 homers in those years, followed by 26 in 2012, giving him nine straight years of 20 or more long balls in a season. After that, his power numbers declined, and in 2014, Konerko retired, having spent sixteen of his eighteen big league years in a White Sox uniform. He ranks number one in team history in total bases, second in home runs, RBIs, games played, extra-base hits and sacrifice flies, third in hits, doubles and at-bats, fourth in runs scored, singles, hit-by-pitch, walks and intentional walks, and ninth in slugging percentage. Konerko also tied a White Sox record in 2011 when he homered in five straight games, putting him in the company of Greg Luzinski, Ron Kittle, Carlos Lee, A.J. Pierzynski and Frank Thomas, who did it twice.

Not only was Konerko a great player, Dawson said he was an even greater person. "He took a lot of pride in the way he played the game. He's not going to do anything to embarrass the franchise, he never did anything to embarrass us as a program. He was always somebody we can be extremely proud of."

Along with being a member of the Chaparral Firebirds Hall of Fame, Konerko was inducted into the Arizona Fall League Hall of Fame in 2011 and the Arizona High School Hall of Fame in 2013. With all the numbers and honors he's accumulated over his Major League career, some people are talking about the possibility of Konerko being inducted into another Hall of Fame.

Its address is 25 Main St., Cooperstown, NY.

Career:
High School: Chaparral (Scottsdale) Class of 1994
MLB: 1997-2014
Clubs: Los Angeles Dodgers (1997-1998); Cincinnati Reds (1998); Chicago White Sox (1999-2014)
Bats: Right
Throws: Right
Games: 2,349
Average: .279
Home Runs: 439
RBIs: 1,412
Hits: 2,340
Runs: 1,162
Doubles: 410
Triples: 8
Strikeouts: 1,391
Walks: 921
Slugging Percentage: .486
On-Base Percentage: .354
Stolen Bases: 9
Fielding Percentage: .995
League Leader Fielding Percentage at 1B: 2003 (.998)
League Leader Double Plays Turned at 1B: 2004 (136), 2005 (135), 2007 (131)
MLB All-Star: 2002, 2005, 2006, 2010, 2011, 2012

Baseball America **Minor League Player of the Year:** 1997
Post-Season Appearances: 2000, 2005, 2008
World Series Championship: 2005
Arizona High School Hall of Fame: 2013

SECOND BASE

Unlike Konerko, this next selection did not have to move to Arizona. Born and raised in Tucson, he was one of the state's top high school players during the closing years of the 20th Century. In the 21st Century, he helped turn the Texas Rangers from perpetual also-rans into one of baseball's elite teams.

His name is Ian Kinsler.

With the help of his father, Howard, who worked as a prison warden, Kinsler honed his baseball skills from an early age. Along with the usual backyard catches, the senior Kinsler also coached his son in little league. Baseball skills were not the only things Kinsler's father instilled in him. He also got some lessons in discipline. Case in point, when Kinsler was 13, his father was giving instructions to their little league team when Kinsler rolled his eyes. Dad did not hesitate in benching son for the entire game.

After little league, it was on to Canyon Del Oro High School. With his bat and speed, he helped lead the Dorados to a pair of state championships in 1997 and his senior year of 2000, when he hit .504 with 26 stolen bases and was selected to the All-State First Team.

His coach at Canyon Del Oro, Kent Winslow, said, "Ian was, without a doubt, one of the most competitive kids I've ever coached. He was very quiet and very straight-faced. He showed hardly any emotion, but when the game was on the line, he was excited about that, and he played very steady and very tough. He was a picture of mental toughness."

One thing that contributed to his mental toughness was never being the best player on his team from little league to high school, and always having to prove himself.

"He grew up with a group of kids that were exceptional," said Winslow. "CDO little league, CDO High School, for a stretch of about ten years, there was nobody in the state as competitive as they were. He grew up in an atmosphere where his little league team had guys that were great players, and he was a little, skinny booger that could play, too, but he wasn't the big basher kind of guy."

Shortly after graduation, Kinsler was drafted by the Arizona Diamondbacks.

In the 29th Round, the 879th pick overall.

Kinsler declined to sign and went the college route.

Despite his success at Canyon Del Oro and being drafted by a Major League team, Kinsler could not catch on with an NCAA D-1 school. Instead, he stayed in his home state and played for Central Arizona College. He put together a big year in 2001, batting .405 with three home runs, 37 RBIs, 17 doubles and 24 stolen bases. That helped the Vaqueros win the conference title, and earned Kinsler a spot on the All-Conference Second Team.

Now the big-time college programs started paying attention to him. More specifically, ASU. Kinsler became a Sun Devil in 2002, and a teammate of future Boston Red Sox star Dustin Pedroia. The plan was to move Pedroia to second base while Kinsler played shortstop. But as the old military axiom goes, "No plan survives first contact with the enemy."

ASU hosted an early season tournament, and as Kinsler said in an August 11th, 2008 article in *Sports Illustrated,* "Four games in four days. I played like crap."

After the tournament, Pedroia was moved to shortstop, and Kinsler was moved to the bench. That's where he spent most of his one and only season at Arizona State.

Kinsler left his native state for the Midwest, where he spent the 2003 season with the University of Missouri. He flourished with the Tigers, batting .335 with six homers, 45 RBIs, 54 runs scored, 13 doubles and 16 stolen bases. Big numbers for a guy who, at the time, wasn't so big. According to Coach Winslow, "He was just a stick, but he had great hands, great bat speed, and he was just a great competitor."

His stats for Mizzou got him a spot on the All Big 12 Second Team. It also got him noticed by the Texas Rangers, who drafted him much higher than the Diamondbacks did.

Kinsler went in the 17th Round, the 496th pick overall.

He was assigned to the Spokane Indians, a short season Single-A squad. His first season as a pro was okay, batting .277 with 15 RBIs, 32 runs scored and 11 stolen bases in 51 games.

The next year, Kinsler did better than okay.

Splitting time between the Single-A Clinton LumberKings and the AA Frisco Roughriders, he hit .345 with 20 home runs, 98 RBIs, 51 doubles, 103 runs scored, 23 stolen bases and a .575 slugging percentage. He garnered all sorts of recognition during that monster season; Midwest League All-Star, *Baseball America* Midwest League Most Exciting Player, Second Team Minor League All-Star, #11 Minor League Prospect, and the Texas Rangers Tom Grieve Minor League Player of the Year Award.

No surprise, Kinsler jumped to AAA in 2005. He continued his torrid hitting for the Oklahoma RedHawks, batting .274 with 23 homers, 94

RBIs, 28 doubles, 102 runs scored and 19 stolen bases. He made the Pacific Coast League All-Star Team and cracked *Baseball America's* Top 100 Prospects list . . . at #98.

In 2006, Kinsler got the call to The Show as the Texas Rangers starting second baseman. After a brief stint on the disabled list, he returned to the line-up and put up impressive numbers in his rookie year. He batted .286 with 14 homers, 55 RBIs, 27 doubles, 65 runs scored and 11 stolen bases, and came in seventh in the AL Rookie of the Year voting.

Over the next several years, Kinsler became one of the top hitters in a very potent Rangers line-up. Defensively, however, he had his issues, including leading American League second sackers in errors five times (2006 with 18, 2007 with 17, 2008 with 18, 2012 with 18 and 2013 with 13). On the flip side, he also led AL second basemen in double plays turned with 123 in 2008 and 103 in 2011.

But it was his stick that got Kinsler notoriety, along with his speed. Kinsler reached the 30-30 club twice, in 2009 with 31 homers and 31 stolen bases, and again in 2011 with 32 homers and 30 steals. That made him only the 12th player in big league history to achieve that feat multiple times. Others in that exclusive club include Willie Mays, Barry Bonds, Bobby Bonds, Jeff Bagwell, Sammy Sosa and Vladimir Guerrero.

That display of speed came as no surprise to Coach Winslow, who said, "He was a fun kid to coach because, aggressive coach that I am, he was your dream. He'd set stuff up for us. He drove high school catchers and pitchers nuts, because if he got on first, you knew he was going to run to second, and he probably stole third more than anyone I've ever coached. He had great instincts."

Kinsler accomplished another rare feat in 2009. In an April 15th contest against the Baltimore Orioles, he hit for the cycle with two singles, two doubles, a triple and a solo home run.

Despite battling injuries in 2010, Kinsler made the American League All-Star team for the second time at that point in his career. He finished the regular season with a .286 batting average, nine homers, 45 RBIs, 20 doubles, 73 runs scored and 15 stolen bases.

Then came the post-season, and that's when he really turned it on.

The Canyon del Oro alum homered and drove in two runs in Game Two of the Divisional Series as Texas topped the Tampa Bay Rays 6-0. In the fifth and deciding game, Kinsler drove in Vlad Guerrero on a groundout in the sixth inning, then smacked a two-run homer in the ninth as Texas got the deke 5-1 to move on to the ALCS. Kinsler drove in three runs in that series as the Rangers defeated the Yankees four games to two to advance to the World Series for the first time in their history.

The Fall Classic, however, would not be kind to Kinsler. He batted just .188 as the Rangers fell to the Giants in five games.

He would have a chance to redeem himself the following year.

After hitting .250 with a homer and three RBIs in the Rangers 3-1 divisional series victory over Tampa Bay, Kinsler became one of

Detroit's biggest nemeses in the 2011 ALCS. He batted .292 with six RBIs, three of them coming in Game Six, as the Rangers bested the Tigers to go to the World Series for the second straight season.

This time on baseball's grand stage, Kinsler did not struggle at the plate. He batted .360 with two RBIs and two runs scored, and was one strike away from a World Series ring when David Freese's two-run triple tied the score at 7-7 in Game Six. After Josh Hamilton's two-run bomb in the top of the tenth gave Texas a 9-7 lead, Kinsler and his teammates were again one out away from a World Championship when, two batters after Ryan Theriot's groundout RBI, Lance Berkman's RBI single tied the game 9-9. In the eleventh, Kinsler watched from second base as Freese launched the ball deep into the night for a walk-off home run and a 10-9 St. Louis victory.

In Game Seven, Kinsler singled twice, but was caught stealing in the first inning and got picked off in the second. St. Louis won 6-2 to claim their eleventh World Championship.

In 2013, Kinsler passed Bump Wills to become the Rangers all-time stolen base leader. He didn't hold it for long, however. On April 18th, 2014, Elvis Andrus overtook him with his 173rd swipe in a Texas uniform.

And Kinsler was nowhere around to get the top spot back.

The November before, he was dealt to the Detroit Tigers for slugger Prince Fielder. Kinsler did take some parting shots at Rangers management in the March 17th, 2014 edition of *ESPN: The Magazine,* saying that the culture of the team had changed. He also accused General Manager Jon Daniels of pushing out CEO Nolan Ryan, whom Kinsler credited with making the Rangers a winning ball club.

The trade turned out to be a blessing for Kinsler. An injury limited Fielder to just a handful of games in 2014. Texas went into a downward spiral, losing 95 games and finishing last in the AL West.

Kinsler, meanwhile, thrived in the Motor City. He batted .275 with 17 home runs, a career-best 92 RBIs, 100 runs scored, 40 doubles, 15 stolen bases and led the league in at-bats with 684. His glove work earned him the Wilson Defensive Player of the Year award for second base. He was also named to his fourth All-Star team, and returned to the post-season. Not that it was a triumphant return. Kinsler went 1-12 and the Tigers wound up getting swept by Baltimore in three games in the ALDS.

After eight seasons with Texas, Kinsler ranks in the top ten in numerous categories. He is number two in stolen bases, number five in runs scored, number six in extra-base hits, number seven in doubles, total bases and walks, number eight in home runs, at-bats and sacrifice flies, number nine in hits and RBIs, and number ten in games played.

In 2013, Kinsler was inducted into the University of Missouri Athletics Hall of Fame. He also found himself on a very unique baseball card. Kinsler was part of the Hank Greenberg 75th Anniversary edition of Jewish Major League Baseball Cards, released in 2008, his first All-Star season.

Career (As of 2014):
High School: Canyon del Oro (Oro Valley) Class of 2000
College: Central Arizona College (2001); Arizona State University (2002); University of Missouri (2003)
MLB: 2006-present
Clubs: Texas Rangers (2006-2013); Detroit Tigers (2014-present)
Bats: Right
Throws: Right
Games: 1,227
Average: .273
Home Runs: 173
RBIs: 631
Hits: 1,333
Runs: 848
Doubles: 289
Triples: 27
Stolen Bases: 187
Slugging Percentage: .449
On-Base Percentage: .344
Strikeouts: 647
Walks: 491
League Leader At-Bats: 2014 (684)
League Leader Double Plays Turned at 2B: 2008 (123), 2011 (103)
MLB All-Star: 2008, 2010, 2012, 2014
Post-Season Appearances: 2010, 2011, 2012, 2014
World Series Appearances: 2010, 2011
University of Missouri Hall of Fame: 2013

SHORTSTOP

This position is also filled by a Tucson native. He started out as one of the top hitting shortstops in the majors, then morphed into one of the top defensive shortstops.

It's J.J. Hardy.

From the time of his birth in 1982, Hardy seemed destined to become a star athlete. His father, Mark, played on the pro tennis circuit before becoming a full-time instructor. His mother, Susie, was one of the top collegiate golfers in the nation. Those are definitely some quality genes, and Hardy put those genes to good use. He was a standout player at Sabino High School, not just at short but also on the mound. Hardy made the All-State team three times – 1999, 2000 and 2001. He even made the roster of the 2001 U.S. Olympic Junior National Team, which won the silver medal.

"He was one of the best athletes, period, I've ever seen," said Michael Hanson, Hardy's coach at Sabino. "On the mound he was 90, 91, but when he fielded the ball at shortstop and threw it across the mound, he was 94."

After graduation, Hardy was offered a scholarship to the UofA, but when the Milwaukee Brewers drafted him the Second Round – 56th overall – he opted to go pro.

The wild success that had been a staple of his high school career did not carry over to the professional ranks. Splitting time in rookie ball between the Ogden Raptors and Arizona League Brewers, Hardy hit .248 with just two homers and 16 RBIs.

The next year, though, he turned into the hitter the Brewers organization expected. Playing for the Single-A High Desert Mavericks, Hardy batted .293 with seven home runs, 48 RBIs, 19 doubles and 53 runs scored in 84 games before being promoted to the AA Huntsville Stars. 2003 was a big year for the former Sabino Sabercat as he posted a .279 average with 12 homers, 62 RBIs, 26 doubles and 67 runs scored. That got him a spot on the Southern League All-Star Team and an invite to that year's MLB All-Star Futures Game. In 2004, Hardy was assigned to the

AAA Indianapolis Indians. Three years after graduating from Sabino, he was just a heartbeat away from the majors.

That's when he suffered a serious shoulder injury.

With his career in jeopardy, Hardy admitted in a March 11th, 2011 *Baltimore Sun* article written by Jeff Zrebiec, "I went into a kind of depression, and never left my house for a long time. I sat in a dark, dark house, my shoulder was broken, and I just was kind of depressed."

J.J. was not the only Hardy battling depression. His brother, Logan, recently returned from the war in Iraq, suffered from post-traumatic stress disorder. The two shared a home in Phoenix, helping one another to recuperate, mentally and physically.

Hardy's shoulder healed. Instead of going back to AAA, he impressed the Brewers so much at spring training that he was named their opening day shortstop.

Year One in the bigs wasn't too bad. Hardy batted .247 with nine homers, 50 RBIs and 46 runs, while committing 10 errors in 402 chances. Year Two, unfortunately, found Hardy dealing with another serious injury. During an early season game against the Philadelphia Phillies, he hurt his ankle sliding into catcher Sal Fasano and required season-ending surgery.

In 2007, Hardy bounced back big time. He batted .277 with 26 homers, 80 RBIs, 30 doubles and 89 walks. He also proved a disciplined hitter, striking out 73 times in 592 at-bats. In the field, he was just as good, committing 13 errors in 578 chances. All of that got Hardy named to his very first All-Star Game.

2008 proved another successful season. Hardy hit .283 with 24 home runs, 74 RBIs, 78 runs scored, and set career highs in doubles with 31 and triples with four. He was a major reason Milwaukee made the post-season for the first time since 1982, when the team was in the American League. While he batted .429 with two RBIs in the National League Divisional Series, most of his Brewer teammates struggled against Philadelphia's pitching and bowed out after four games. The Phillies, meanwhile, went on to win the World Series.

All the success the Brewers, and Hardy, had did not spill over into 2009. A combination of free agent departures and injures resulted in Milwaukee struggling just to hover around the .500 mark. Hardy was not immune to those struggles. Going into the middle of August, he was hitting just .229 with 11 homers and 45 RBIs. In a major personnel shake-up, General Manager Doug Melvin fired pitching coach Bill Castro, who had been with the club for 18 years, cut infielder Bill Hall and sent Hardy to AAA Nashville. In November of that year, Milwaukee shipped Hardy to Minnesota for outfielder Carlos Gomez. He was bit again by the injury bug as a left wrist contusion limited him to 101 games. Hardy hit .268 with six homers and 38 RBIs in the regular season. His post-season numbers couldn't have been worse. Hardy hit an even .100 as the Twins were swept in the ALDS by the New York Yankees. There would be no season two in Minnesota for the Sabino grad as he and infielder Brendan Harris were sent to the Baltimore Orioles for a pair of minor league pitchers, Jim Hoey and fellow Arizonan Brett Jacobson. A graduate of Cactus Shadows High School in Cave Creek, Jacobson compiled an 18-18 record with a 4.50 ERA and nine saves in six minor league seasons.

The change of scenery worked wonders for Hardy. Despite an early season injury that kept him out of action for much of April, he wound up hitting .269 with 30 home runs, 80 RBIs, 27 doubles and 76 runs scored. He also led all AL shortstops in fielding percentage at .990.

In 2012, Hardy's average dropped to .238 and he had a career high in strikeouts with 106. Still, he belted 22 home runs, drove in 68 runs, scored 85 runs and hit 30 doubles. His fielding got even better. Hardy committed only six errors in 779 chances and once again led AL shortstops in fielding percentage at .992. That earned him his first career Gold Glove.

"The one thing where J.J. always excelled is, he would separate the offense from the defense," said Hanson. "You could always count on him to go out and play great defense."

Hardy's defense was a big reason the Orioles qualified for the post-season for the first time since 1997. In the Wild Card Game versus Texas, Hardy got Baltimore on the board in the first inning with an RBI single off Yu Darvish. The Orioles went on to beat the defending American League champs 5-1 and move on to the ALDS versus the New York Yankees. Hardy struggled throughout the series, batting just .136 as the Pinstripes knocked out Baltimore in five games.

He came back in 2013 with a big year both at the plate and in the field. Hardy batted .263 with 25 home runs, 76 RBIs, 27 doubles and 66 runs scored. Not only was he selected to his second All-Star Game, this time as the starting shortstop, he also won his second career Gold Glove and received a Silver Slugger Award as the best hitting shortstop in the American League.

The recognition of Hardy's defense was something Hanson felt was long overdue. "He was always on the cusp of that, I thought. If you go back and look at his days with the Brewers, and his one year with the Twins, and then with the Orioles, they were always better defensively when he was at shortstop. He was always at the right place at the right time, making all the routine plays, every once in a while making a web gem. That's just maturity. He got into his pro prime while he was at Baltimore."

Hanson recalled when Hardy was at Sabino, "We hit him hundreds and hundreds of fungos, and my son, who was three years ahead of him, said, 'I could just sit here and watch him take grounders all day long.' He's just so fluid, he just does everything right."

Hampered by injuries, Hardy's production dipped in 2014. He batted .268 with nine homers, 52 RBIs, 56 runs scored and 28 doubles. His offense did perk up in the post-season as he homered in Game One of the ALDS against Ian Kinsler's Detroit Tigers, which Baltimore won 12-3. In Game Two, Hardy had an RBI single off Justin Verlander in the fourth inning to inch the Orioles closer to the Tigers 5-3. Then in the eighth, Hardy walked to load the bases and scored the eventual game-winning run on Delmon Young's pinch-hit double as Baltimore triumphed 7-6 and went on to sweep Detroit. But in the ALCS, Hardy's bat was stymied by Kansas City pitching. He hit .200 and drove in one run as the Orioles were swept by the Royals.

Not that this should come as a surprise, considering his father's profession, but Hardy still has a great love for tennis. In a June 20th, 2012 interview on the U.S. Tennis Association's website, Hardy said he built a tennis court at his house to use during the off-season and named Andy Roddick, Pete Sampras and Ana Ivanovic among his favorite players.

Career (as of 2014):
High School: Sabino (Tucson) Class of 2001
MLB: 2005-present
Clubs: Milwaukee Brewers (2005-2009); Minnesota Twins (2010); Baltimore Orioles (2011-present)
Bats: Right
Throws: Right
Games: 1,259
Average: .261
Home Runs: 167
RBIs: 579
Hits: 1,234
Runs: 606
Doubles: 235
Triples: 13
Slugging Percentage: .422
On-Base Percentage: .312
Stolen Bases: 8
Strikeouts: 756
Walks: 353
Fielding Percentage: .982
League Leader Fielding Percentage by Shortstop: 2011 (.990), 2012 (.992)
League Leader Assists by Shortstop: 2012 (529)
League Leader Double Plays Turned by Shortstop: 2012 (113), 2013 (108)
MLB All-Star: 2007, 2013
Gold Gloves: 2012, 2013, 2014
Post-Season Appearances: 2008, 2010, 2012, 2014

THIRD BASE

How do you know you're really good? When the Major League team that drafts you says, "Forget about the minors. We need you in the big leagues right now."

That's what happened with the starting third baseman for Arizona's All-Time Baseball Team, Bob Horner.

The future slugger took a roundabout path to become an Arizona resident. He was born in Junction City, Kansas in 1957. His family moved to the Los Angeles area, then in 1971 came to Glendale. Horner enrolled at the brand new Apollo High School and right off the bat – no pun intended – showed everyone his athletic prowess by starting for the varsity basketball team as a freshman. While he was a good basketball player, he excelled for the Hawks baseball team. So much so when he graduated in 1975, he was drafted in the 15th Round, 357th overall, by the Oakland A's. Horner declined their offer and opted to play at Arizona State University. On the day he signed, it was not then-Sun Devil Coach Jim Brock who picked up Horner's paperwork, it was Brock's wife, Pat.

She explained her husband was at Los Angeles International Airport that day. "He called me from a payphone from the airport to tell me that the flight was on time and that I was to pick him up at the airport, and he was really down because he hadn't signed anybody. Just after we hung up, the phone rang again, and it was Jim Horner, Bobby Horner's father. He asked if he could speak to Jim and I explained he was in California, but he'd be home soon and I could ask him to call as soon as he got back in town. And he said, 'Oh no, that's all right. I can talk to him tomorrow. It's just that, Bobby's going to go to ASU and he's ready to sign his form.' And I said, 'Great, will he sign it tonight?'"

Jimmy Horner asked his son that question, to which the younger Horner replied, "Sure."

Pat responded, "I'll be right out. He said, 'But it's raining cats and dogs out there,' and I said, 'I don't care. This will make my husband's day."

Pat Brock said when she presented Jim Brock with Horner's letter of intent and scholarship offer, it put a smile on his face.

Coach Brock smiled a lot during Horner's time at ASU, as the Apollo grad put together one of the greatest careers in collegiate baseball history.

In his first season with the Sun Devils, Horner hit .339 with nine home runs and 42 RBIs, made the All WAC Team and helped ASU to a third place finish at the College World Series.

His second season for the Sun Devils was outstanding. He wore out college pitchers with a .389 average and led the entire nation in both home runs with 22 and RBIs with 87. Once again, he made the All WAC Team and led Arizona State to the College World Series. In six games in Omaha, Horner batted .444 with two bombs and nine RBIs as the Sun Devils won their fourth National Championship. He was named the MVP of the College World Series and received First Team All-American honors.

His third season for the Sun Devils was one of the most legendary in college baseball history.

Horner hit .412 with 25 homers and 100 RBIs. As you'd expect, he took home an armful of awards. His third All WAC Team honor, another First Team All-American honor, *The Sporting News* College Player of the Year award and the first ever Golden Spikes Award for the best player in college baseball. ASU also went to the College World Series again, but this time finished as National Runners-Up. Horner ended up with 56 career home runs, still the all-time Sun Devil record.

In the 1978 MLB Draft, Horner was taken by the Atlanta Braves in the first round as the number one pick overall. At the time, the Braves were languishing in the National League West cellar. Figuring they had nothing to lose, they skipped over the whole work-your-way-up-through-the-minors thing and immediately put Horner in the majors. That made him one of just twenty-one players to go from the draft right to The Show. Some of the others who did that are former Diamondback Mike Morgan, former Blue Jay John Olerud, ASU products Eddie Bane and Mike Leake, and Hall of Famer Dave Winfield.

Less than two weeks after being drafted, Horner found himself in a Braves uniform at Atlanta's Fulton County Stadium facing the Pittsburgh Pirates. If the Major League atmosphere intimidated him, it didn't show. Horner celebrated his professional debut by going deep off future Hall of Famer Bert Blyleven. Not that it helped the Braves as they lost 9-4. In fact, after three years of playing for a championship caliber team at ASU, Horner found himself part of one of the worst teams in the majors. Atlanta finished with a 69-93 record, dead last in the NL West.

While the Braves stunk, Horner didn't. He batted .266 with 23 homers, 63 RBIs, 17 doubles and 50 runs scored in 89 games. Despite only playing half the season, Horner was voted the 1978 National League Rookie of the Year.

1979 saw no sophomore slump for the Apollo alum. Horner had career highs in batting average (.314) and RBIs (98) while belting 33 home runs. Atlanta, however, endured another losing season at 66-94.

The Braves steadily improved over the next couple of years, with it all coming together in 1982. Horner hit .261 with 32 home runs, 97 RBIs, 24 doubles and 85 runs scored. Not only did it earn him the one and only All-Star selection of his career, it also helped Atlanta win its first NL West title since 1969. Unfortunately, they were stymied by the eventual World Champion St. Louis Cardinals in the NLCS. Horner especially, as he hit .091 and watched his Braves get swept in three games.

Things got worse from there for Horner.

He broke his right wrist late in the 1983 season, missing the Braves final 43 games.

He broke his right wrist early in the 1984 season, and did not play the rest of the year.

Horner healed up and came back with a vengeance. He put together solid seasons in 1985 and 1986, with 27 homers both years and 89 and 87 RBIs respectively. That '86 season also saw him become the 11th player in baseball history to smack four home runs in one game. Would you believe, however, even with that performance, the Braves still lost 11-8 to the Montreal Expos. That made Horner the second player in history, along with Phillies Hall of Famer Ed Delahanty, to hit four homers in a game for a losing team.

Just when it looked like things were back on track, Horner became one of the many victims of the collusion scandal. In order to reduce the length and price of contracts, many owners agreed not to pursue top players once their contracts expired. Despite the numbers he put up his previous two years, no MLB team was willing to sign Horner for the 1987 season.

Instead, the former Sun Devil journeyed across the Pacific to continue his baseball career. In April of 1987, Horner signed with the Yakult Swallows of Nippon Professional Baseball. Japan proved very, very good to Bob Horner as he batted .327 with 31 homers, 73 RBIs and 60 runs scored.

The following year, Horner found a Major League team interested in him. The St. Louis Cardinals, who came within one win of the 1987 World Championship, needed a power hitter to replace the departed Jack Clark. They felt Horner was their man.

That didn't work out as planned.

Horner played just 60 games for the Cards, hitting .257 with three homers and 33 RBIs before a shoulder injury sidelined him for the rest of the 1988 season. He tried to make a comeback with the Baltimore Orioles in 1989, but his shoulder was still not fully healed. On March 9th, Horner announced his retirement at the age of 31.

In a May 7th, 2010 article in the *Atlanta Journal-Constitution* written by Ken Sugiura, Horner, looking back on his career, said, "I had a great time. I lived a dream. I wouldn't trade it for anything in the world. I made some great friends, fabulous people who to this day I call friends. My regret is that you have a couple of injuries, and it cuts short a couple of things you'd like to have done. You start going down that road, it serves no purpose. It is what it is"

As of 2014, Horner ranks seventh in home runs and ninth in slugging percentage on the Braves all-time list.

If there was one drawback to Horner, it was his defense. He was not blessed with great speed or range, and wound up with a career fielding percentage of .946 splitting time between third base and first base. But what he lacked in his glove work he more than made up for with his bat work, and it's a tradeoff any team can live with. Especially since Horner was not one of those sluggers who racked up an insanely large number of strikeouts. The most times he ever fanned in a season was 1982, when he heard that "strike three" call just 75 times.

Long after his career ended, Horner continued to garner honors and awards. In 1994, he was named to *Baseball America's* All-Time College All-Star Team. In 1999, he was selected to another *Baseball America* All-Time team, the College Player of the Century Team. Horner came in at #2 on that list. That same year, *Sports Illustrated* put him at #36 on their list of Arizona's Greatest Sports Figures.

The honors didn't stop there. In 2002, he was one of eleven players named to the 25th Anniversary Golden Spikes Team. In 2006, he was inducted into the College Baseball Hall of Fame. Horner got another Hall of Fame plaque in 2009, this one for the Arizona High School Sports Hall of Fame. And for good measure, he was named one of *Sports Illustrated's* 50 Best College Athletes of All Time.

During his ten seasons in the majors, Horner's power only abandoned him during one particular situation. When the bases were loaded. Horner had one single, solitary grand slam, and it didn't come until his final season with the Braves. On September 6th, 1986, Horner took Pittsburgh rookie starter Stan Fansler deep, plating himself, Glenn Hubbard, Omar Moreno and Ken Oberkfell for Atlanta's only runs of the game, which was enough as they beat the Pirates 4-2. At the time, Horner had the record for most career home runs without a grand slam at 210. That record stood until 1998 when it was broken by none other than Sammy Sosa.

Career:
High School: Apollo (Glendale) Class of 1975
College: ASU (1976-1978)
MLB: 1978-1986, 1988
Clubs: Atlanta Braves (1978-1986); St. Louis Cardinals (1988)
Bats: Right
Throws: Right
Games: 1,020
Average: .277
Home Runs: 218
RBIs: 685
Hits: 1,047

Runs: 560
Doubles: 169
Triples: 8
Slugging Percentage: .499
On-Base Percentage: .340
Strikeouts: 512
Walks: 369
Stolen Bases: 14
MLB All-Star: 1982
NL Rookie of the Year: 1978
Post-Season Appearance: 1982
Golden Spikes Award: 1978
ASU Hall of Fame: 1979
College Baseball Hall of Fame: 2006
Arizona High School Sports Hall of Fame: 2009

OUTFIELD

The first starting outfielder for Arizona's All-Time Baseball Team is someone whose family is no stranger to success on the diamond. His father Byron played for Yavapai College when they won a JUCO National Championship in 1977, and the son became an all-star player in the big leagues.

He's Andre Ethier, and he's the starting left fielder.

Granted, Ethier has spent most of his time with the Dodgers in right field, but he is no stranger to left, having played there over 200 times during his major league career. Since I have someone else in mind for right field, Ethier gets moved to the other side of the outfield.

Born in Phoenix, Ethier was an explosive hitter throughout his little league career. His bat didn't cool off when he got to high school. During his senior year in 2000, he hit over .500 for St. Mary's and made the All-Region First Team and All-State Second Team. ASU offered him a full-ride, and Ethier was ready to fulfill his lifelong dream, to play for the Sun Devils.

The dream, however, crumbled in a hurry.

After Arizona State's fall season, Head Coach Pat Murphy told Ethier he was not ready to play at the Division One level, and should seek out another school. In a July 13th, 2010 ESPN Los Angeles.com article by Tony Jackson, Ethier said, "At the time, it was sort of a big shock. It had been a dream of mine to go to school there, play there and start there. To have someone take that away from you and say you're not good enough, it's a blow. But at the same time, you sit back and take a look at the situation, and you realize it's not the end of the world. I ultimately decided to just look at it as a challenge, something I had to overcome."

He rose to that challenge by putting up huge numbers for Chandler-Gilbert Community College. Ethier batted .468 with 32 doubles in 2001. Along with being named the team MVP, he was also selected to the All Conference First Team and named a Junior College All-American. That put him on the radar screen of the Oakland A's, who drafted him in the 37th Round. It also put him back on Coach Murphy's radar screen as he invited him back to ASU. Thus, it was take two of Andre Ethier's dream to be a Sun Devil.

This time, he would live that dream to its fullest.

In two seasons at Arizona State, Ethier compiled a .371 average with 14 home runs, 118 RBIs, 27 doubles, 113 runs scored and a .559 slugging percentage. He made the All Pac-10 Team twice, was named All-American Honorable Mention by CollegeBaseballInsider.com, and was voted ASU's most outstanding defensive player. His 2002 season was highlighted by a pair of five RBI games, the first vs. St. John's, the second vs. Washington State.

Ethier's stock went up in the eyes of Oakland management. In 2003 they drafted him in the Second Round, 62nd overall, and sent him to Canada to begin his professional career. Ethier spent only ten games with the Single A Vancouver Canadians, but what a ten-game stretch it was. He batted .390 with a home run, seven RBIs, seven runs scored and four doubles. Oakland brought him back to the U.S. to play for another Single A team, the Kane County Cougars. Ethier came back down to earth in Illinois, batting .272 with 11 RBIs, 23 runs scored and ten doubles in 40 games.

In 2004, Ethier made the jump to advanced Single A, suiting up for the Modesto A's. He batted .313 with seven home runs, 53 RBIs, 72 runs scored and 23 doubles. Those numbers would have been bigger had it not been for a back injury that ended his season after 99 games and kept him from playing in the post-season, which saw Modesto win the California League Championship.

The injury, however, did not keep him from being promoted to the AA Midland RockHounds in 2005. It was in Texas that Ethier would have a career year. He hit .319 with 18 homers, 80 RBIs, 104 runs scored, 31 doubles and a .384 on-base percentage. He was named the Texas League Player of the Year, the Oakland A's Minor League Player of the Year and the MVP of the Texas League All-Star Game. Ethier, however, did not get to participate with the RockHounds in the post-season, which saw them capture the Texas League Championship, as he ended the 2005 season with the AAA Sacramento River Cats. Still, he seemed poised to become a huge star for the Athletics.

Milton Bradley, however, changed all that.

Mounting issues between the Dodger outfielder, teammates and management convinced the L.A. front office it was time to part ways with Bradley. He was sent to Oakland, along with reserve infielder Antonio Perez. In return, the A's sent Ethier to the Dodgers.

The trade turned out to be a blessing in disguise for him. He began the 2006 season with the AAA Las Vegas 51s and only spent a month with them, batting .349, before getting the call to The Show. Ethier's big league debut on May 2nd was certainly a special one, as the Dodgers happened to be in his hometown of Phoenix to play the Diamondbacks. After going 0-

3, Ethier came up in the top of the seventh and smacked a double to right field for his first Major League hit.

The ex-Sun Devil had a very solid first year for the Dodgers, hitting .308 with 11 homers, 55 RBIs, 20 doubles, seven triples and 50 runs scored. He was also named the National League Player of the Week for July 9th and voted to the 2006 Topps All-Star Rookie Team.

After a pretty good 2007 (.284, 13 HR, 64 RBIs), Ethier really found his power stroke. In 2008, he batted .305 with 20 homers, 77 RBIs, 90 runs scored and 38 doubles.

That was nothing compared to what he'd do in 2009.

Ethier achieved career highs in a number of offensive categories. Home runs with 31, RBIs with 106, doubles with 42 and runs scored with 92. That earned him a Silver Slugger award as one of the best hitting outfielders in the NL. He also made up for his lack of post-season production the season before. In the 2009 National League Divisional Series vs. St. Louis, Ethier belted homers in Games Two and Three as L.A. swept the Cardinals. In the NLCS vs. Philadelphia, Ethier hit .263 with a home run, three RBIs and two runs scored, but it wasn't enough as the Phils beat the Dodgers four games to one to advance to the World Series.

Just when it looked like Los Angeles was about to become one of the elite teams in the National League, with Ethier as one of its star players, everything fell apart. The public divorce of team owner Frank McCourt and team CEO Jamie McCourt took its toll on the Dodgers. There were issues with team payroll. Ownership of the Dodgers was in dispute. The drama apparently affected the players on the field as L.A. finished 4th in 2010 and 3rd in 2011.

Ethier persevered through it. Despite an injury in 2010, he hit .292 with 23 homers, 82 RBIs, 71 runs scored and 33 doubles, and was named to his first All-Star team. He also hit .292 in 2011, was selected to the All-Star team again, and won his first Gold Glove, but his power numbers dropped off. Ethier had 11 homers, 62 RBIs, 67 runs scored and 30 doubles. He attributed this to a knee problem, which had started two years before and had gotten worse during 2011, forcing him to sit out the final month of the season.

Ethier bounced back in 2012, batting .272 with 20 homers, 89 RBIs, 79 runs scored and 36 doubles. As you've probably gathered already, this guy is a veritable doubles machine. From 2007-2013, Ethier hit 30 or more doubles every season. But don't think this St. Mary's alum is all about hitting. Ethier has turned into one of the top defensive outfielders in baseball. Want proof? How many players can claim to go an entire season without committing an error? Andre Ethier can. In 2011, he committed ZERO errors in 126 games. Ethier also showed off his incredible defensive skills in 2010 with just one error in 132 games and two errors in both 2008 and 2013. In addition, he racked up double-digit assists in 2007 (10) and 2008 (11).

Once the McCourt soap opera was settled and new ownership took control, the Dodgers again become one of baseball's top teams, winning NL West titles in 2013 and 2014.

That team success did not translate to individual success at the plate for Ethier. While he batted .272 in 2013, his power numbers dropped to 12 home runs and 52 RBIs. 2014 was even worse as he batted a career low .249 with just four homers and 42 RBIs. His defense, though, didn't suffer, as he committed only one error in 92 games in the outfield and had a fielding percentage of .992.

One thing that has been a constant throughout Ethier's career is the fiery intensity. Boston Red Sox second baseman Dustin Pedroia, who was Ethier's teammate at ASU, said in the ESPN Los Angeles.com article referenced earlier, "He is that intense because he wants to win and he wants to do a good job. That's a good thing. I will take a guy any time who gets mad because he didn't get a hit."

In 2010, Ethier was named to the ASU All-Decade Team. That same year, his uniform number at St. Mary's High School was retired.

Along with piling up doubles, Ethier has another specialty. Walk-off hits. In 2009, he had six of them, including on consecutive nights June 5th and 6th versus the Phillies, a game-ending double off Brad Lidge, followed the next night by a walk-off solo home run off Chad Durbin.

Career:
High School: St. Mary's (Phoenix) Class of 2000
College: Chandler-Gilbert Community College (2001); ASU (2002-2003)
MLB: 2006-present
Clubs: Los Angeles Dodgers (2006-present)
Bats: Left
Throws: Left
Games: 1,275
Average: .285
Home Runs: 145
RBIs: 629
Hits: 1,238
Runs: 582
Doubles: 281
Triples: 27
Stolen Bases: 27
Slugging Percentage: .462
On-Base Percentage: .359
Strikeouts: 847
Walks: 470
Fielding Percentage: .987
Assists: 61
Gold Glove: 2011
MLB All-Star: 2010, 2011

League Leader Fielding Percentage OF: 2011 (1.000)
League Leader Double Plays turned from OF: 2013 (4)
Post-Season Appearances: 2006, 2008, 2009, 2013, 2014

This next player is not only the starting center fielder for Arizona's All-Time Baseball Team, he's also the sort of speedy guy you want at the top of the batting order.

He is Billy Hatcher.

Growing up in Williams along the famous Route 66, Hatcher was one of the top athletes at Williams High School. Not just in baseball, but football, basketball and track and field. That made for a busy school year for him. In a September 16th, 1993 Los Angeles Times article by Chris Dufresne, a former high school teammate of Hatcher's detailed a day in 1979 when Hatcher took part in a baseball playoff game and the state track and field finals at the same time.

"You could hear the loudspeakers for both events. (Hatcher) would get up to bat, play an inning, switch clothes, jump a 6-foot fence and run track in 105-degree heat. He won the state one hundred. He'd run back and forth between innings. He did in one day what would be unheard of for us."

Hatcher netted all-state honors in all four sports he played. Following his phenomenal high school career, he had an exceptional career for Yavapai College in Prescott. His coach there, Rod Soesbe, said of Hatcher's athleticism, "The first time I saw Billy was actually on a basketball court, and to be able to, at 5'8, take one step and dunk the ball with two hands, really showed his athletic ability. He was just a tremendous athlete as far as his running speed. He wasn't a real plus arm, but I think the strongest thing he had was not just his athletic ability, but his attitude, his desire, and enjoyment playing the game."

During his time at Yavapai, Hatcher was named a Junior College All-American in 1980 and 1981, as well as the Conference Player of the Year in '81. Soesbe summed up Hatcher like this, "Talking to [Billy's] high school coach a year after he played for me, I said if you had nine Billy Hatchers you could win any national championship. And he says, 'Coach, you're just fortunate to have one like Billy Hatcher.' That's always stuck with me, him saying that, because you are fortunate to have a young man like that. Not only with the athletic ability, but with the type of person he is."

There would be no transferring to a four-year school for Hatcher upon graduation. The Chicago Cubs drafted him in the Sixth Round, 131st overall, and assigned him to the Geneva Cubs of the short-season Single A New York-Penn League. He had a pretty good first season as a pro, batting .280 with four homers, 40 RBIs, 57 runs scored, 15 doubles and 13 stolen bases.

His second season as a pro was outstanding.

Playing for the Salinas Spurs, Hatcher hit .311 and was second in the California League in steals with 84. He was beaten out for the stolen base crown by Mike Felder, who went on to a ten-year Major League career with the Brewers, Giants, Mariners and Astros. Hatcher also had eight homers, 59 RBIs, 92 runs scored, 18 doubles and eight triples and struck out just 47 times in 549 at-bats. No surprise, he jumped to AA in 1983 with the Midland Cubs. While his average dropped a bit to .299, Hatcher's other offensive numbers went up. He had ten home runs, 80 RBIs, 33 doubles, 11 triples and a Texas League-leading 132 runs scored. He also came in third in stolen bases with 56. Who came in first? Would you believe it was, once again, Mike Felder with 71.

Next up was AAA, as Hatcher started the 1984 season with the Iowa Cubs. Again he put up impressive numbers with a .276 average, nine homers, 59 RBIs, 96 runs scored, 27 doubles, a .340 on-base percentage, and was second in the American Association in triples with 18 and stolen bases 56. He was just one triple away from the league leader, Daryl Boston, who played 11 seasons in MLB. As for stolen bases, Hatcher was a very distant second to a man who was one of the premier base stealers of the 1980s, future St. Louis Cardinal Vince Coleman, who had 101 swipes for the Louisville Redbirds.

Coach Soesbe explained what made Hatcher such a great base runner. "His speed was one thing, but his aggressiveness along with that, and his intelligence as he grew with the game. He could pick his spots and you could give him spots to run. He just worked on that part of the game, and he ran hard all the time."

Hatcher earned a September call up in 1984, appearing in eight games for the Chicago Cubs, batting .111 with two stolen bases. In 1985, he split time with the Cubs in Iowa and the Cubs in Chicago, appearing in 53 games in The Show, batting .245 with just two stolen bases. After the season, the Cubs looked to strengthen their outfield by trading Hatcher to the Houston Astros for Jerry Mumphrey, who was coming off an All-Star season. As it turned out, the trade helped Houston more than it helped Chicago. The Cubs went 70-90 and finished 5th in the NL East. The Astros, meanwhile, went 96-66 and won the NL West title, thanks in part to Hatcher. As the starting center fielder, he hit .258 with six home runs, 36 RBIs, 55 runs scored, 38 stolen bases, 15 doubles, four triples and a .302 on-base percentage. He also proved a solid fielder as he put up a .983 fielding percentage with just four errors in 237 chances. But it was in the NLCS where he made a name for himself on the national stage. He batted .280 in the series versus the New York Mets, and had a memorable hit in one of the most memorable playoff games in baseball history.

Game Six, October 15th, 1986. The Astros, who were on the brink of elimination, took a 3-0 lead in the first inning, with Hatcher scoring one of those runs. That score stood until the ninth inning when the Mets came back to tie the game. New York took the lead in the top of the fourteenth on a Wally Backman RBI single. In the bottom of the inning, Houston was two outs away from the end of their season when Hatcher came to the plate. He smacked a fly ball down the left field line and jogged backwards toward first base, watching, hoping for the ball to stay fair.

It did! Hatcher's solo shot tied the game 4-4.

Unfortunately, it only delayed the inevitable. The Mets plated three runs in the top of the sixteenth. The Astros made a valiant comeback in the bottom of the frame, with Hatcher driving in Davey Lopes with an RBI single to make it a 7-5 game. Glenn Davis's single plated Bill Doran to make it a 7-6 game, but Jesse Orosco's strikeout of Kevin Bass ended Houston's, and Hatcher's, dreams of trip to the World Series.

1987 was Hatcher's most productive big league season. He achieved career highs in batting average at .296, home runs with 11, RBIs with 63, runs scored with 96, doubles with 28 and stolen bases with 53, which was the third most in the National League behind Tony Gwynn's 56 and Vince Coleman's 109. Houston, however, did not return to the post season as they went 76-86 and ended up third in the NL West.

Hatcher spent another season-and-a-half in Houston before he was dealt to the Pittsburgh Pirates in August of 1989 for Glenn Wilson. His stay in the Steel City lasted just 27 games. Prior to the start of the 1990 season, Hatcher was dealt to the Cincinnati Reds for Jeff Richardson and Mike Roesler, both of whom played a grand total of 96 big league games. With All-Star Eric Davis entrenched in center field, Hatcher was moved to left field. He had a pretty good regular season with a .276 average, five homers, 25 RBIs, 68 runs scored and 30 stolen bases. Cincinnati won the NL West with a 91-71 record and met the Pittsburgh Pirates in the League Championship Series.

Hatcher's bat really came alive in the post-season. He hit .333 with a two-run bomb in the second inning of Game Three to put the Reds on top 2-0. They went on to win the game 6-3 and ultimately take the NLCS four games to two. Unlike in 1986, Hatcher would play in a World Series, and had one of the greatest performances in the history of the Fall Classic.

The Oakland A's came into the series the heavy favorites. They were, after all, the defending World Champions, won 103 games in the regular season and easily dispatched the Boston Red Sox in a four-game sweep in the ALCS.

None of that intimidated Billy Hatcher. All he did was set a World Series record with mind-blowing batting average of .750. He went 9-for-12 at the plate with two walks, four doubles, two RBIs and six runs scored. The Reds swept the A's in four games for their first World Championship since 1976. Despite his record-setting performance, Hatcher was not named the series MVP. That went to pitcher Jose Rijo, who won two of the four games, fanned 14 and had a miniscule 0.59 ERA.

Hatcher remained with the Reds until 1992, then signed as a free agent with the Boston Red Sox. He had a pretty good 1993 season, hitting .287 with nine home runs, 57 RBIs, 71 runs scored and 24 doubles, but only seven stolen bases. His production declined sharply in 1994, hitting .245 between the Red Sox and the Philadelphia Phillies with just 31 RBIs and 39 runs scored. Hatcher tried to reverse his fortunes with the Texas

Rangers in 1995, but was released after hitting .083 in six games. He signed with the Kansas City Royals, who assigned him to their AAA club in Omaha, where one-time Major League stars like Vince Coleman, Harold Reynolds and Kevin Elster were also trying to make comebacks.

Hatcher never made it to the Royals. He played 26 games for Omaha, batting .276. Following the 1995 season, he retired at age 34, ending a twelve-year Major League playing career.

Hatcher remained in baseball, serving as a coach for the Tampa Bay Devil Rays from 1998-2005 before being hired as a coach by the Cincinnati Reds from 2006 to the present. He was selected #41 on *Sports Illustrated's* 1999 list of Arizona's Greatest Sports Figures and was inducted into the Yavapai College sports Hall of Fame in 2014.

Besides his speed, another aspect of Hatcher's game that makes him the perfect leadoff man for Arizona's All-Time Baseball Team is his plate discipline. During his Major League career, he never struck 100 times. The most strikeouts he ever amassed in a single season was 70 in 1987. Even though he never won a Gold Glove, you couldn't ask for a better defender in center than Hatcher. He had a career .986 fielding percentage, committing 33 errors in 2,389 chances. He also racked up 67 career assists, including a single-season high 16 in 1987.

Hatcher's athleticism was also passed down to his children. His son, Derek, was the 2004 Class A football Player of the Year in Florida and went on to help the University of Richmond win the NCAA Football Championship Subdivision national title in 2008 with 334 punt return yards, four interceptions – two of them returned for touchdowns – and 84 tackles. Daughter Chelsea had a successful soccer career for the University of Tennessee, with 16 goals and 11 assists for 43 points. She was also named to the All SEC First Team and National Soccer Coaches Association of America's All-South Region Team her junior year of 2010.

Career:
High School: Williams, Class of 1979
College: Yavapai Community College (1980-1981)
MLB: 1984-1995
Clubs: Chicago Cubs (1984-1985); Houston Astros (1986-1989); Pittsburgh Pirates (1989); Cincinnati Reds (1990-1992); Boston Red Sox (1992-1994); Philadelphia Phillies (1994); Texas Rangers (1995)
Bats: Right
Throws: Right
Games: 1,233
Average: .264
Home Runs: 54
RBIs: 399
Hits: 1,146
Runs: 586
Doubles: 210
Triples: 30

Stolen Bases: 218
Slugging Percentage: .364
On-Base Percentage: .312
Strikeouts: 476
Walks: 267
Fielding Percentage: .986
NL League Leader Fielding Percentage as OF: 1990 (.997)
NL League Leader Double Plays Turned from OF: 1987 (6)
Post-Season Appearances: 1986, 1990
World Series Championship: 1990
Yavapai College Hall of Fame: 2014

Rounding out the outfield of Arizona's All-Time Baseball Team is a man many fans in Anaheim consider the greatest player in the history of the California/Anaheim/Los Angeles Angels. He's known as the Kingfish among Halos fans and "Sockeye" by ESPN commentator Chris Berman.

Starting in right field is Tim Salmon.

Born in Long Beach, California in 1968, Salmon and his family moved to Phoenix, where he became a star player for Greenway High School's football, basketball and baseball teams. On the diamond, he batted .381 with an astounding .905 slugging percentage his senior season, which earned him All-State honors. One reason for his success was his work ethic, as Greenway's coach at the time, Ted Blake, remembers.

"He was one of these guys who'd go through a pair of batting gloves in a week. He'd stay after [practice], saying, 'Coach, can you throw more BP.' He was always putting the time and effort in, and he never big leagued anybody. He was never cocky, he was never, 'It's all about me.' He was a team guy, and he was probably as nice a young man as we've had at the program."

Upon his graduation in 1986, he was drafted by the Atlanta Braves in the 18th Round, 450th overall. The 17-year-old Salmon, however, elected not to sign and play for Grand Canyon University. All he did there was put up gaudy numbers. In three seasons with the Antelopes, Salmon slugged 51 home runs and scored 225 runs – both still all-time team records – had the third most career RBIs with 192 and the third best career batting average at .383. He was drafted again after his junior season, this time by the California Angels in the Third Round, 69th overall. Salmon decided to forego his senior season and turn pro.

His first two years in the minors were all right. Salmon batted .245 with six homers and 31 RBIs in 55 games for the Single-A Bend Bucks in 1989. The next year, he hit a combined .279 with five home runs and 37 RBIs in 63 games for the Single-A Palm Springs Angels and the AA Midland Angels.

In 1991, Salmon's batting average dropped to .245. His other offensive numbers, however, went up dramatically. Salmon hit 23 home runs, the third most in the Texas League, while driving in 94 runs and scoring 100 runs. He also added 26 doubles, four triples and 12 stolen bases to his stat line. That earned him a promotion to AAA for the 1992 season, and it was in Edmonton where he turned into an offensive juggernaut. Salmon led the Pacific Coast League in home runs, RBIs, on-base percentage and slugging percentage with 29, 105, .469 and .672 respectively. He also tied for first with future Indian and Dodger Wayne Kirby in runs scored with 101, was third in batting average at .347 and third in doubles with 38. He was not only the clear choice for league MVP, but was named *Baseball America's* Minor League Player of the Year.

California didn't even wait for September. They called up Salmon in late August and had him start 21 games in right field. He batted just .177 and drove in six runs.

Things got better for Salmon in 1993. Much, much better. He upped his average to .283, socking 31 home runs with 95 RBIs, 93 runs scored and 35 doubles. That made him the unanimous choice for AL Rookie of the Year. Following the strike shortened 1994 season, Salmon hit 30 or more homers, drove in 98 or more runs and scored 90 or more runs from 1995-1997. In two of those years, '95 and '97, he had 105 and 129 RBIs respectively, the latter his career high. He also established career highs in batting average and runs with .330 and 111 respectively. Salmon earned a Silver Slugger Award as one of the top hitting outfielders in 1995.

His production slipped a bit in 1998. While hitting .300, Salmon had 26 homers and 88 RBIs. A wrist injury limited him to 98 games in 1999, but he bounced back in 2000 to bat .290 with 34 homers, 97 RBIs, 108 runs scored and 36 doubles.

Just when it seemed the former Antelope was back on track, he suffered his worst season in the big leagues.

In 2001, injuries reared their ugly head again. Issues with his foot, wrist, groin and shoulder contributed to his stats taking a nosedive. He hit .227 with 17 home runs and 49 RBIs. His struggles continued the first month of the 2002 season, as Salmon batted just .192 in April. Some reporters and analysts were talking retirement for the now 32-year-old outfielder. Perhaps many other players would have hung it up. But Salmon's Christian faith got him through all the adversity. It paid off as not only he, but the Anaheim Angels, had a memorable season.

Salmon put his April struggles far behind him and ended the 2002 regular season with a .286 batting average, 22 homers, 88 RBIs, 84 runs scored, a career-high 37 doubles and a .503 slugging percentage. That got him named the AL Comeback Player of the Year.

That wasn't even the best part of Salmon's season. For the first time in his major league career, he took part in the post-season, and made the most of it.

Salmon terrorized the New York Yankees in the ALDS. With the Halos down 6-1 in the third inning of Game Three, he smacked a two-run double off Mike Mussina to cut the deficit in half. Then in the eighth, with Anaheim leading 7-6, Salmon provided them with a little more breathing room with a 2-run jack. The Angels held on to win 9-6, with Salmon posting four RBIs in the game. The next day, he had an RBI single in Anaheim's eight-run fifth inning as they defeated the Yanks 9-5 to take the series 3-1. Salmon ended up batting .263 with two homers, seven RBIs and three runs scored in the ALDS. The Angels went on to beat Minnesota in five games in the AL Championship Series, but Salmon was a non-factor, batting .214 with no home runs and no RBIs.

He made up for that big time in the Angels first ever World Series.

After losing Game One to the San Francisco Giants, both teams engaged in a slugfest in Game Two, and Salmon was front and center for the all the fireworks. He blasted two homers, including a two-run jack in the eighth inning that broke a 9-9 tie, and helped the Halos win 11-10. Salmon went on to bat .346 in the World Series with two homers, five RBIs and seven runs scored as Anaheim beat the Giants in seven games to win their first, and at the present time only, World Championship.

2003 was another productive season for Salmon, as he hit .275 with 19 home runs, 72 RBIs, 78 runs scored and 35 doubles. After that, the injury bug struck with a vengeance. Salmon played in just 60 games in 2004 and missed all of 2005. He returned in 2006, playing the majority of his 76 games as a DH, and hit .265 with nine homers and 27 RBIs. Shortly before the season ended, Salmon announced his retirement, ending a fourteen-year MLB career, all of it with the Angels.

Blake said there was a time when Salmon almost wore another uniform. "He had an opportunity, at one time, to come to the Diamondbacks. I don't know how far it went, but his major concern was he really thought it would be cool to start and finish your career with one team. That was big on his mind."

Salmon has kept himself busy in his post-baseball life. He is involved with many charities and faith-based organizations, and has coached his children's sports teams. He is also still active with the Angels as part of their broadcast team for FOX Sports West.

Salmon's baseball legacy endures from high school to the pros. Greenway High School retired his number in 2005. He was inducted into the Grand Canyon University Hall of Fame in 2010 and donated funds to his alma mater to build a new clubhouse for the baseball team. Two years later, he was inducted into the Arizona Sports Hall of Fame. The SB Nation fan site "Halos Heaven" named Salmon the number one Angels player of all-time, and deservedly so. He is the team's all-time leader in home runs and walks, second in RBIs, hits, runs scored, doubles, games played, total bases and at-bats, and third in on-base percentage and slugging percentage.

Coach Blake said this about Salmon's career with the Angels. "He was the epitome of a professional athlete. He was never in trouble, never argued too much. He did get tossed in one game, and was so embarrassed. He was great for that community. It doesn't surprise me that he was voted the most popular Angel of all time."

In spite of all his accomplishments, one honor eluded Salmon during his Major League career. He was never named to an All-Star team.

Career:
High School: Greenway High School (Phoenix) Class of 1986
College: Grand Canyon University (1987-1989)
MLB: 1992-2006
Clubs: California/Anaheim/Los Angeles Angels (1992-2006)
Bats: Right
Throws: Right
Games: 1,672
Average: .282
Home Runs: 299
RBIs: 1,016
Hits: 1,674
Runs: 986
Doubles: 339
Triples: 24
Slugging Percentage: .498
On-Base Percentage: .385
Stolen Bases: 48
Strikeouts: 1,360
Walks: 970
Fielding Percentage: .978
League Leader Assists by RF: 1997 (15)
AL Rookie of the Year: 1993
Baseball America's **Minor League Player of the Year:** 1992
Post-Season Appearance: 2002
World Series Champion: 2002
Arizona Sports Hall of Fame: 2012
Grand Canyon University Hall of Fame: 2010

CATCHER

There's a glut of good ones vying for this position. Paul Lo Duca was a standout player at Apollo High School, a Golden Spikes Award finalist at ASU and a four-time MLB All-Star. Ozzie Virgil was a second-generation player who went from Phoenix's Moon Valley High School to All-Star seasons for both the Phillies and the Braves. Ron Hassey helped lead Tucson High School to the 1972 State Championship and UofA to the 1976 National Title before embarking on a 14-year big league career.

But the man who gets the nod as the starting backstop for Arizona's All-Time Baseball Team is a Tucson native who had a lifetime batting average of .253 and never had more than 60 RBIs in any of his twelve MLB seasons. On the other hand, he was one of the top defensive catchers of the 1990s, and given all the offensive threats already on this team, we can afford to go with more of a glove man at this position.

Rounding out the starting eight is Tom Pagnozzi.

A star player for Rincon High School, he set a single-season record for batting average his senior year at .548. That got him selected to the All-City Team and the Arizona Super Team. It also got him a spot on the Central Arizona College baseball team. In his two years with the Vaqueros, Pagnozzi batted .412 (seventh all-time) with 11 home runs, 149 hits (third all-time), 106 runs scored (tied eighth all-time), 26 doubles and eight triples. He was named to the All-Conference Team in 1981 and received a Junior College All-American Honorable Mention in 1982. Following his sophomore season, he was drafted by the Milwaukee Brewers, but did not sign, opting instead to play at the University of Arkansas. It was during his time as a Razorback that he began his transition from third base to catcher.

"I'd never caught in my life," Pagnozzi said in a January 12th, 2008 interview with Terrell Lester of the *Claremore Daily Progress.* "I didn't measure up in pro ball as an everyday third baseman because I didn't run well and I wasn't going to go out and hit 30 home runs. That was the prototype that they were looking for."

Luckily for Pagnozzi, one of Arkansas's assistant coaches was Dave Ricketts, a back-up catcher for the St. Louis Cardinals from 1963-1969. The ex-Redbird laid the foundation for Pagnozzi to become a catcher, but he required more work after being selected in the Eighth Round, 208th overall, by St. Louis in the 1983 Draft. While he batted .293 in 63 games with the Erie Cardinals and the Macon Redbirds, he committed 11 errors behind the plate.

But Pagnozzi would not be deterred. He went to winter ball in order to get more experience. In 1984 for the Single-A Springfield Cardinals, he batted .283 with ten homers and 68 RBIs, but committed 12 errors.

Pagnozzi recalled in the *Claremore Daily Progress* interview, "I'm 21, and I'm starting to learn something new. It wasn't easy. I was really learning on the fly."

So he went back to winter ball. The philosophy of, "You get better through repetition" came true for Pagnozzi. In 89 games for the AA Arkansas Travelers and AAA Louisville Redbirds in 1985, he committed just five errors and had a fielding percentage of .991. He began the 1987 season with St. Louis, but ended up spending most of that year in Louisville, where he hit .313 with 14 home runs, 71 RBIs and a .989 fielding percentage. That impressed the Cards enough to include him on their post-season roster.

After beating the San Francisco Giants in seven games in the NLCS, St. Louis went to the World Series to face the Minnesota Twins. The 24-year-old Pagnozzi was penciled into the starting line-up for Game One as the designated hitter. He went 1-3 with a single as St. Louis got pummeled 10-1. Pagnozzi wouldn't see action again until Game Six as a pinch hitter in the fifth inning, flying out to right field, but advancing Ozzie Smith to third. The Wizard scored on a Willie McGee single, increasing the Cardinal lead to 5-2. The Twins, however, staged a massive rally to win 11-5 and force a Game Seven at the Metrodome. Pagnozzi spent that deciding game on the bench and watched the Cardinals fall to Minnesota 4-2.

With Tony Pena the starting catcher and up-and-coming Todd Zeile his heir apparent, Pagnozzi was relegated to the bench from 1988-1990. The Cards struggles in '90 led to the firing of Whitey Herzog, who had helmed the team during the entire decade of the 80s. He was replaced briefly by Cardinal legend Red Schoendienst, who was then replaced by Joe Torre. His arrival would signal a turnaround of Pagnozzi's fortunes.

Wanting to take advantage of Zeile's power, Torre moved him to third base. Finally, Pagnozzi got his shot as the starting catcher. What did he do with this opportunity? He won back-to-back Gold Gloves in 1991 and 1992 and was named to his only All-Star team in '92. He also led the National League in throwing out baserunners, gunning down 70 in 1991. In 1992, he led the league in fielding percentage among catchers with an incredible .999. That got him voted the league's top defensive catcher in a *Baseball America* poll. In another poll by *Baseball Digest,* Pagnozzi was voted by NL managers as the league's best throwing catcher. His .998

fielding percentage in 1994 was also tops among NL catchers. That same year, he threw out 50% of baserunners trying to steal on him.

In 1996, along with having another solid defensive season with a .990 fielding percentage, Pagnozzi had the best offensive year of his big league career. He hit .270 with 13 homers, 55 RBIs, 23 doubles and 48 runs scored. That carried over into the National League Divisional Series versus San Diego, where he batted .273 with two big RBIs. The first came in Game Two, when his groundout in the eighth inning plated Brian Jordan for the game-winning run in the Cards' 5-4 victory. In Game Three, Pagnozzi's single in the sixth inning scored John Mabry with the tying run. St. Louis went on to win 7-5 and sweep San Diego. In the NLCS versus Atlanta, Pagnozzi's bat went ice cold. He hit .158 as the Cards lost in seven games.

The next two seasons saw Pagnozzi spend more time on the disabled list than in the field. Injuries to his calf, hip and shoulder limited him to a combined 76 games in 1997 and 1998. St. Louis released Pagnozzi before the end of the '98 season. Shortly after, he retired, having spent his entire twelve-year MLB career in a Cardinal uniform.

A year after hanging up his cleats and catcher's mask, Pagnozzi was inducted into both the Pima County Sports Hall of Fame and the Arkansas Letterman's Association Hall of Honor. He also came in at #24 on *Sports Illustrated's* list of Arizona's Greatest Sports Figures. In 2010, he was inducted into the Missouri Sports Hall of Fame. Now residing in the Fayetteville area, Pagnozzi gives back to his former university, having served as a volunteer assistant coach, and forming Pagnozzi Charities to support the Razorback baseball team.

Career:
High School: Rincon (Tucson) Class of 1980
Colleges: Central Arizona College (1981-1982); University of Arkansas (1983)
MLB: 1987-1998
Clubs: St. Louis Cardinals (1987-1998)
Bats: Right
Throws: Right
Games: 927
Average: .253
Home Runs: 44
RBIs: 320
Hits: 733
Runs: 247
Doubles: 153
Triples: 11
Slugging Percentage: .359
On-Base Percentage: .299
Stolen Bases: 18
Strikeouts: 450

Walks: 189
Fielding Percentage: .992
Runners Caught Stealing: 293
League Leader Runners Caught Stealing: 1991 (70)
League Leader Fielding Percentage as C: 1992 (.999), 1994 (.998)
Gold Gloves: 1991, 1992, 1994
MLB All-Star: 1992
Post-Season Appearances: 1987, 1996
World Series Appearance: 1987
University of Arkansas Letterman's Association Hall of Honor: 1999
Pima County Sports Hall of Fame: 1999
Missouri Sports Hall of Fame: 2010

THE STARTING ROTATION

We have our starting line-up for Arizona's All-Time Baseball Team, now it's time to pick the five pitchers who will make up the starting rotation. Over fifty natives and transplants have toed the rubber in the bigs. Some have had great careers, some have been pretty good, some not so good, and others came and went like a shooting star in the Arizona night. These include players like Harqua Hala native Flame Delhi and Tucson High grad Chris Saenz, who pitched only one major league game each, with very opposite results. Saenz's appearance came on April 24th, 2004 when he threw six shutout innings, striking out seven and picking up the win in the Milwaukee Brewers 3-1 triumph over the St. Louis Cardinals. Delhi, on the other hand, was shelled by Detroit in his Major League debut on April 16th , 1912, little over two months after Arizona officially became a state. He allowed six runs, three earned, on seven hits and three walks in three innings of work as the Chicago White Sox fell to the Tigers 10-1.

Needless to say, neither Saenz nor Delhi made this team. We're looking for pitchers who had a lot more experience, and a lot more success, at the big league level. At the top of that list is the only player with roots in Arizona who is enshrined in Cooperstown, a man who left the Big Apple for the Grand Canyon State, then went back east to become one of the most dominant pitchers of the 1970s.

That man is Jim Palmer.

Born in New York in 1945, the infant Palmer was adopted by garment industry executive Moe Wiesen and his wife Polly. Wiesen passed away when Palmer was nine and the family moved to Beverly Hills, where Polly later married Max Palmer, an actor and professional wrestler whose film credits include *Invaders from Mars* and *Killer Ape.* The family moved again shortly before Palmer began high school, this time to Arizona. That's where he showed off his athletic prowess, earning all-state honors at Scottsdale High School not just in baseball, but in basketball and football.

After going 10-0 his senior year in 1963, he was recruited by several big-time colleges, including Stanford and USC. UCLA showed interest in Palmer, but not for baseball. Legendary coach John Wooden wanted him for the Bruins basketball team. Had he accepted the offer, Palmer could have played on three national championship teams (1964, 1965 and 1967) and been teammates with 1963-1964 Player of the Year Walt Hazzard and Lew Alcindor, better known as Hall of Famer Kareem Abdul-Jabbar. Instead, Palmer opted to go pro, signing a $50,000 contract with the Baltimore Orioles, a pretty tidy sum back then.

It turned out he was worth the price. Assigned to the Aberdeen Pheasants of the Single-A Northern League, the 18-year-old Palmer went 11-3 with a 2.51 ERA, while the team ended up with an astounding record of 80-37. The next season, he made the jump from the low minors all the way to the Baltimore Orioles.

Palmer's rookie year, however, was nothing to get excited over. He spent much of his time in the bullpen and started only six of the 27 games he appeared in. Still, he ended up with a respectable 5-4 record, a 3.72 ERA, 75 strikeouts and 56 walks in 92 innings of work.

In 1966, Palmer started to show the makings of an ace. At 19 years of age, he led Orioles pitchers in wins with 15, and had the second most strikeouts and innings pitched on the staff with 147 and 208 respectively. Baltimore wound up 97-63, won the American League pennant and faced the Los Angeles Dodgers in the World Series.

The O's took Game One 5-2. Palmer got the nod for Game Two. His opponent on the mound? None other than future Hall of Famer Sandy Koufax, who led the National League that year with 27 wins, 317 strikeouts and a 1.73 ERA, and garnered his third Cy Young Award.

Baseball's biggest stage, featuring one of the greatest pitchers of that era, did not intimidate Palmer. He threw a gem, going the distance, allowing no runs and four hits while striking out six. Koufax only lasted six innings as Baltimore got the win 6-0. It should be noted that those runs were not all Koufax's fault. The Dodgers put on one of the worst displays of defense in World Series history, committing six errors, which led to three unearned runs. Also of note, Koufax retired before the 1967 season due to elbow problems. That means Palmer has the distinction of beating Koufax in his very last Major League appearance.

Baltimore swept the Dodgers in four games and Palmer won his first World Series ring six days shy of his 20th birthday. Everything seemed to be falling into place for him to become one of the game's premier pitchers.

But in 1967, Palmer's career took a huge step backwards. Arm and shoulder problems limited him to nine games. He spent the entire 1968 season in the minors, trying to recover from his injuries. Palmer pitched in only 10 games that year, going 0-2. Many felt his promising career was over, so much so he was not protected by the Orioles for the American League expansion draft. Neither of the new franchises, the Kansas City

Royals nor the Seattle Pilots – who became the Milwaukee Brewers in 1970 – selected Palmer. There are probably people in both KC and the City of Suds still crying, "Why? Why?" over that.

Palmer recovered from his ailments and went 16-4 with a 2.34 ERA and 123 strikeouts in 1969, a season highlighted by a no-hitter versus Oakland on August 13th. Baltimore won the AL East title and Palmer got the start in Game Three of the ALCS. While Minnesota touched him up for ten hits, he allowed only two runs and struck out four through nine innings. His teammates gave him plenty of run support as the Orioles won 11-2 to finish off the Twins and move on to the World Series.

It was a Fall Classic that would not be kind to Palmer. With the series tied 1-1, he started Game Three versus "The Amazin' Mets." The very first batter he faced, Tommy Agee, blasted the ball over the center field fence at Shea Stadium. It was all downhill from there as Palmer lasted six innings, giving up four runs, five hits, four walks and striking out five. The O's lost the game 5-0, and ultimately lost the series four games to one.

1970 was a much better season for the Scottsdale High grad. Palmer went 20-10 with a 2.71 ERA and a career-high 199 strikeouts. He also led the AL in innings pitched with 305 and shutouts with five, and was the starting pitcher for the American League in the All-Star Game, where he threw three effective innings, allowing one hit and striking out three. He even swung a decent stick, hitting .150 with a home run and nine RBIs. The Orioles dominated the AL East, going 108-54 and winning the division by 15 games over the New York Yankees. They had a rematch in the ALCS with the Twins, and swept them again, with Palmer putting on a show in Game Three. He went the distance, giving up one run and seven hits while striking out 12. He also helped his cause with an RBI double off Bert Blyleven in the third inning as the Orioles finished off the series with a 6-1 victory.

At age 24, Palmer found himself in his third World Series, this time against the Cincinnati Reds, who went 102-60. He was the Game One starter and got roughed up early as Cincy led 3-0 after three innings. Baltimore rallied to take the lead and Palmer, helped out by reliever Pete Richert, shut down the Reds offense to get the win 4-3.

Palmer came back to pitch Game Four, the day before his 25th birthday, with a chance to close out the series in Baltimore's favor. However, he struggled throughout the game, pitching seven innings and allowing five runs on six hits, including a home run to Pete Rose. He also walked four and struck out seven. Palmer was relieved in the eighth inning by Eddie Watt, with the O's holding a 5-3 lead over the Reds. But the first batter Watt faced, Lee May, blasted a three-run homer which turned out to be the game-winning hit, final score Cincinnati 6, Baltimore 5.

That only delayed the inevitable. Palmer celebrated his birthday on October 15th, 1970 by watching the Orioles beat the Reds 9-3 to win the World Series, earning him his second championship ring.

1971 saw Palmer as part of one of the most successful rotations in Major League history. He, Mike Cuellar and Pat Dobson won 20 games apiece, with Dave McNally winning 21. No surprise, Baltimore captured its third straight league championship, then faced the up-and-coming Oakland A's in the ALCS. Palmer, yet again, was the Game Three starter and, yet again, threw a complete game victory to close out the playoffs and move on to his fourth World Series.

After Baltimore won Game One, Palmer started Game Two. While he walked eight batters, he did strike out ten, with the only damage coming from Richie Hebner's three-run bomb in the eighth. The Orioles went on a tear at the plate and trounced the Bucs 11-3 to go up two games to none in the series. Palmer also contributed offensively. Even though he didn't get a hit, he walked with the bases loaded not once, but twice!

Palmer took the bump again in a critical Game Six. After losing the first two games, the Pirates took the next three at Three Rivers Stadium and were one win away from the world championship.

Palmer got off to a rough start as Pittsburgh led 2-0 after three innings. But he settled down and shut them out through the next six innings before being relieved by Pat Dobson. Brooks Robinson's sac fly in the tenth plated Frank Robinson to give Baltimore the 3-2 win and tie the series at three-all. But in Game Seven, Steve Blass outdueled Mike Cuellar and the Pirates won 2-1 for their fourth World Series title.

Palmer's dominance continued in 1972 and 1973 with 21 and 22 wins respectively. He also led the AL with a 2.40 ERA and won his first Cy Young Award in 1973. Baltimore won the Eastern Division and took on the defending world champs, Oakland, in the league championship series. Palmer was tapped as the Game One starter and silenced the A's formidable offense, allowing no runs on five hits and five walks while striking out 12 in a complete game 6-0 win.

Game Four, however, was a complete 180 for Palmer. He got touched up for three early runs, and with Baltimore down two games to one, manager Earl Weaver was not going to take any chances. He replaced Palmer in the second inning with Bob Reynolds. The bullpen stymied the A's the rest of the way while home runs by Andy Etchebarren and Bobby Grich gave the O's the 5-4 win and tied the series at two-all. Palmer came back the next day for Game Five to relieve starter Doyle Alexander, who gave up three runs to Oakland. While Palmer pitched four shutout innings, Baltimore's offense could do nothing against future Hall of Famer Catfish Hunter as the A's won 3-0 and went on to beat the Mets for their second straight world championship.

Arm troubles plagued Palmer throughout 1974. He posted a 7-12 record with a 3.27 ERA with 84 strikeouts in 178 innings. Even without their ace pitching like an ace, the Orioles still won the AL East crown by two games over the Yankees. Once again, they met the Oakland A's in the ALCS. Palmer put aside his struggles during the regular season and pitched a near masterpiece, giving up just one run, four hits and a walk while striking out four in nine innings. The A's Vida Blue, however, was better that day. He threw a two-hitter, fanning seven, as Oakland edged out Baltimore 1-0. The A's took the series, then beat the Dodgers in five games for their third consecutive world title.

Palmer returned to form the next season, and the season after that, and the season after that, and the season after that. From 1975-1978, he won 20 or more games, leading the AL in wins in '75, '76 and '77. He was also the league leader in innings pitched three times during that span and led the AL in ERA at 2.09 and shutouts with ten in 1975. That earned him All-Star selections in 1975, 1977 and 1978, and two more Cy Youngs in '75 and '76. Palmer also showed he was no slouch at fielding his position as he won Gold Gloves in 1976, 1977 and 1978.

That wild success came to a halt in 1979. Arm soreness landed Palmer on the disabled list twice. Still, he went 10-6 with a 3.30 ERA and won his fourth straight Gold Glove. As in 1974, Palmer's down year did not prevent Baltimore from winning the AL East, this time with a record of 102-57.

Palmer got the start in Game One of the ALCS versus the California Angels. After stumbling out of the gate and letting the Halos go up 2-0 in the third inning, he settled down for the next six innings, leaving in the ninth with the score tied 3-3. John Lowenstein's pinch-hit three-run walk-off homer in the tenth gave Baltimore the 6-3 win. The O's went on to beat California in four games. That set up a rematch of the 1971 Fall Classic between Baltimore and Pittsburgh.

The Orioles took Game One 5-4. Palmer got the call in Game Two and gave up two second inning runs. He pitched shutout ball until he was relieved in the 8th, but Baltimore came up short 3-2. Palmer had a chance to redeem himself in Game Six. With the Orioles up three games to two, he and the Pirates John Candelaria both hung bagels on the board through six innings. But Pittsburgh got Palmer for two runs in the seventh and two more in the eighth, while the O's could do nothing offensively and lost 4-0. Baltimore also lost Game Seven, after having a three games to one advantage over the Bucs.

Even though he did not get another World Series ring, the '70s was one heck of a decade for Palmer. He was MLB's winningest pitcher with 186 victories and had eight seasons of 20 wins or more, along with three Cy Youngs, six All-Star appearances, four Gold Gloves, three World Series appearances and one World Championship.

Palmer's effectiveness diminished during the 1980s. After going 16-10 with a 3.98 ERA in 1980 and 7-8 with a 3.75 ERA in the strike-shortened season of 1981, he rebounded in 1982 with a 15-5 record and a 3.13 ERA and came close to winning his fourth Cy Young Award, but wound up second in the voting behind Milwaukee's Pete Vuckovich.

Injuries cropped up again in 1983, limiting Palmer to just fourteen games. After seeing no action in the ALCS versus the Chicago White Sox, he pitched two innings of relief in Game Three of the World Series versus the Philadelphia Phillies, getting the decision in the Orioles 3-2 victory. Baltimore took the series in five games and Palmer earned his third championship ring. That gave him the distinction of being the only pitcher in baseball history to win World Series games in three different decades.

1984 would be the end of the line for Palmer. He pitched in only five games, going 0-3 with a 9.17 ERA before Baltimore released him in mid-May, ending a nineteen-year Major League career.

Palmer had no trouble staying busy after retirement. Most of his post-pitching years were spent as a broadcaster for ABC and the Orioles. He also authored a book titled *Together we were Eleven Foot Nine* about his relationship with long-time manager Earl Weaver.

In 1990, Palmer received baseball's highest honor. He was inducted into the Hall of Fame in his first year of eligibility. His plaque in Cooperstown reads, "Intensity was trademark of 3-time Cy Young winner, who combined strength, intelligence, competitiveness and consistency to become Orioles all-time winningest hurler."

A year after making the Hall, Palmer still felt he had something left in the tank and tried to make a comeback at age 45. He went to spring training with Baltimore, but a hamstring injury quickly put an end to a post-Hall of Fame stint in the majors. Still, Palmer left an indelible legacy not just with the Orioles, but with the game in general. He is number one on Baltimore's all-time list in wins, strikeouts, innings pitched, complete games, games pitched, games started and shutouts. Former Orioles pitching coach Ray Miller called Palmer, "The greatest situation pitcher I've ever seen. He makes them beat him on a single and one run at a time. Most of the homers he gives up are solo because he only works to their power when the bases are empty."

In 1999, *The Sporting News* named Palmer #62 on their list of the 100 Greatest Baseball Players, while *Sports Illustrated* selected him as Arizona's #1 Athlete of all time. He was also named the *Arizona Republic's* #11 Athlete of the Century and inducted into the azcentral.com High School Hall of Fame in 2008. As of 2014, he is number 53 on MLB's all-time strikeout list, 31st in wins, tied for 13th with Gaylord Perry for shutouts and 43rd in innings pitched. Another distinction for Palmer, even though he gave up a fair number of home runs in his career, 303 to be exact, he never allowed a grand slam.

During the 1970s, TV viewers not only saw Palmer in an Orioles uniform, they also regularly saw him without it. He was featured in several commercials modeling Jockey Underwear.

Career:
High School: Scottsdale, Class of 1963
MLB: 1965-1967, 1969-1984
Club: Baltimore Orioles
Throws: Right
Bats: Right
Record: 268-152
ERA: 2.86

Strikeouts: 2,212
Walks: 1,311
Shutouts: 53
Games: 558
Innings Pitched: 3,948
Complete Games: 211
League Leader Wins: 1975 (23), 1976 (22), 1977 (20)
League Leader ERA: 1973 (2.40), 1975 (2.09)
League Leader Shutouts: 1970 (5), 1975 (10)
League Leader Complete Games: 1977 (20)
League Leader Innings Pitched: 1970 (305), 1976 (315), 1977 (319), 1978 (296)
Cy Young: 1973, 1975, 1976
MLB All-Star: 1970, 1971, 1972, 1975, 1977, 1978
Gold Gloves: 1976, 1977, 1978, 1979
Post Season Appearances: 1966, 1969, 1970, 1971, 1973, 1974, 1979, 1983
World Series Appearances: 1966, 1969, 1970, 1971, 1979, 1983
World Series Championships: 1966, 1970, 1983
Inducted into Baseball Hall of Fame: 1990
azcentral.com High School Hall of Fame: 2008

The number two man in the rotation is a pitcher who not only played high school and college ball in Arizona, but also major league ball. He was one of the most prepared, and one of the most outspoken, hurlers during the 1990s and 2000s.

He is Curt Schilling.

Like Palmer, Schilling is not native to Arizona. He came from a climate the complete opposite of the Grand Canyon State. That would be Anchorage, Alaska. In fact, Schilling is one of only eleven native Alaskans to ever play in the majors.

During his youth, Schilling's family moved to several different states before finally settling in Phoenix. Despite showing some promise on the diamond, Schill did not make the Shadow Mountain High School varsity baseball roster until his senior year. After graduating in 1985, he committed to Yavapai College and helped them make it to the 1986 Junior College World Series. The Boston Red Sox thought so much of him they selected him in the Second Round of the MLB Draft, 39th overall. He had a decent first year in the pros, going 7-3 for the Single-A Elmira Pioneers with a 2.59 ERA, two complete games, 75 strikeouts and 30 walks in 93 innings of work. The next season with the Greensboro Hornets was both good and bad. The good? Schilling fanned 189 batters and threw three shutouts and seven complete games. The bad? His record was 8-15.

During the latter part of the 1988 season, with the Red Sox in the midst of a pennant race, Schilling and up-and-coming outfielder Brady Anderson were traded to the down-on-their-luck Orioles for Mike Boddicker, a 20-game winner four years prior. Schill was soon called up to the big club, but went 0-3 with a 9.82 ERA. After three unremarkable seasons with Baltimore, Schilling was part of a huge deal that sent him, pitcher Pete Harnisch and future Diamondback Steve Finley to the Houston Astros for All-Star first baseman Glenn Davis. Used exclusively as a reliever, Schilling went 3-5 with a 3.81 ERA, eight saves, 71 strikeouts and 39 walks in 75 innings of work. However, that would be his only year in Houston. Prior to the start of the 1992 season, Schilling was traded to the Philadelphia Phillies for pitcher Jason Grimsley. Grimsley never pitched a single inning for the Astros, and spent the next decade-and-a-half bouncing from team to team, including the D-backs, going 42-58 with a 4.77 ERA for his career.

Schilling, however, did much, much better during that span.

Splitting his time between starting and relieving, he put up a 14-11 record for the Phils with a 2.35 ERA, four shutouts, ten complete games, two saves, 147 strikeouts and 59 walks in 226 innings of work. The next season, he worked exclusively as a starter and earned national attention.

Comprised of cast-offs, misfits and unknowns, the 1993 Phillies stunned everyone when they won the NL East crown. Despite a 4.02 ERA, Schilling won 16 games, struck out 186 batters, completed seven games and pitched two shutouts. He also got the nod to start Game One of the NLCS versus the heavily favored Atlanta Braves. Schilling threw eight effective innings, striking out ten and giving up seven hits. He left with a 3-2 lead, only to watch Mitch "Wild Thing" Williams blow the save in the ninth when Bill Pecota scored on a groundout to tie the game. Luckily, Kim Batiste's walk-off double in the tenth won it for the Phils.

Game Five was practically a repeat of Game One. Schilling again pitched eight effective innings, left with the lead, watched Williams blow the save, and watched the Phillies win it in the tenth inning. In two playoff games, Schilling had a 1.69 ERA and 19 strikeouts, but was 0-0. Still, when Philadelphia wrapped up the series in Game Six, Schilling was named the Most Valuable Player of the NLCS.

Next it was on to the World Series versus the defending champs, the Toronto Blue Jays. Schilling got the ball for Game One, but got shelled and lost 8-5. He rebounded in Game Five, striking out six and giving up five hits for a 2-0 complete game victory. But thanks to Joe Carter's walk-off, series-winning home run off Williams in Game Six, there would be no World Championship ring for Schilling, or anyone else on the Phils.

His mastery from the '93 post-season did not carry over to 1994, or 1995, or 1996. He went a combined 18-23 over those three years. Schilling got back on track in 1997, going 17-11 with a 2.97 ERA, a league-leading 319 strikeouts, 58 walks, 254 innings pitched and seven complete games. He also earned a spot on the NL All-Star Team and threw two shutout innings, fanning three, though the American League came out on top 3-1.

Schilling was also an All-Star in 1998, when he won 15 games and led the NL in strikeouts with 300, innings pitched with 268 and complete games with seven. In his third All-Star year of 1999, Schilling went 15-6 with a 3.54 ERA, though injuries limited him to 180 innings pitched and 152 strikeouts.

The dawn of the new century saw Schilling return home to Arizona. In a major transaction, the Diamondbacks sent four players to Philadelphia for the Shadow Mountain graduate. Those four were pitchers Omar Daal, Nelson Figueroa and Vincente Padilla, and first baseman Travis Lee. Seems a lot to give up for one man, even a three-time All-Star. But both Daal and Figueroa were gone from Philadelphia by 2002, Padilla went 49-49 in six seasons with Philly and Lee had two fairly productive years in the City of Brotherly Love before moving on to the Devil Rays and the Yankees.

Considering what Schilling would do for the D-backs, giving up those four was a bargain.

In his first full season for Arizona, Schilling led the NL in wins with 22, innings pitched with 256 and complete games with six while striking out 293 and earning his fourth All-Star selection. The Diamondbacks also won the Western Division title and took on the St. Louis Cardinals in the divisional series. Starting Game One, Schilling owned the Redbirds, striking out nine and scattering three hits for a complete game 1-0 win. He also got the start for the deciding Game Five, again going the distance with nine strikeouts as Arizona won 2-1 to advance to the NLCS versus Atlanta. Just like in 1993, Schilling dominated the Braves in the post-season. He threw another complete game, striking out 12 while allowing just one run and four hits as the D-backs won Game Three 5-1. Schilling even helped his own cause with a single and a run scored. Arizona went on to eliminate the Braves in five games.

For the first time ever, the World Series would be played in Arizona. Facing the D-backs was the team that had won more World Championships than any other in baseball, including four of the previous five. The New York Yankees.

The vaunted Pinstripe offense could do nothing against Schill in Game One. He allowed one run on three hits while fanning eight through seven innings as Arizona pummeled New York 9-1. Schilling also pitched well in Game Four in The Bronx, giving up a run and three hits while striking out nine in seven innings. He left with a 3-1 lead, but the win would be denied him. Byung-Hyun Kim gave up a two-run homer to Tino Martinez in the ninth to tie the game, then served up a solo shot to Derek Jeter in the tenth for a walk-off 4-3 Yankees win.

The next time Schilling took the mound, everything was on the line. He went up against the Yankees Roger Clemens in Game Seven at Bank One Ballpark. The two matched each other pitch for pitch, with Schill fanning nine and The Rocket punching out ten. Neither factored in the decision as Clemens was relieved in the seventh and Schilling got taken out in the eighth. Unlike in 1993, Schilling did not have to suffer through his team losing the World Series on a walk-off hit. Down 2-1 in the ninth, the Diamondbacks rallied, and Luis Gonzalez's bloop single to center plated Jay Bell to give them the 3-2 win and the state's first – and to date only – world championship in any of the four major sports leagues. Along with his first World Series ring, Schilling got another piece of hardware, the World Series MVP, which he shared with teammate Randy Johnson.

2002 was another huge season for Schilling. His 23 wins and 316 K's were both second in the NL to Johnson, who won 24 games and fanned 334. The Big Unit also picked up the Cy Young Award, with Schilling the runner-up. Injuries limited his playing time in 2003 to 24 starts and an 8-9 record. In November of that year, Schilling was involved in another four-for-one deal as the Boston Red Sox sent pitchers Brandon Lyon, Casey Fossum, Jorge De La Rosa and outfielder Mike Goss to Arizona for the transplant from Alaska. How did that trade work out? Well, De La Rosa was part of a multi-player deal just days later with the Brewers that gained Arizona slugging first baseman Richie Sexson, who spent most of 2004 on the DL and signed with Seattle the next season. Fossum went 4-15 in his one and only season with the Diamondbacks, Lyon went 11-15 during his four years in the desert, and Goss never made it beyond AA ball.

Schilling, meanwhile, made history.

He led the American League with 21 wins and went to the All-Star Game for the sixth time in his career. He also helped the Red Sox capture the Wild Card and started Game One of the ALDS versus the Anaheim Angels. With massive run support, Schilling allowed three runs in 6 2/3 innings as the Sox got the deke 9-3. Boston swept the series in three games and set the stage for one of the most dramatic post-season contests in baseball history.

The ALCS saw the game's greatest rivalry renewed, as well as a rematch of last year's league championship series. The Boston Red Sox versus the New York Yankees. After Aaron (Bleeping) Boone's walk-off home run broke the hearts of Red Sox Nation in 2003, both fans and players were aching for revenge against their nemesis. Could Curt Schilling deliver for the Fenway Faithful?

He sure didn't in Game One. The Yanks lit him up, chasing him out of the game in the third inning en route to a 10-7 victory. The next two games were also losses for the Sox, including a 19-8 nightmare in Game Three.

Just when it looked like the Curse of the Bambino would remain intact, David Ortiz had back-to-back extra-inning walk-off home runs in Games Four and Five. Schilling got the call for Game Six, which gave us one of the most famous articles of clothing in baseball history.

The bloody sock.

For most people, a dislocated ankle tendon would have them laid up in bed. Not Schilling. He had it sutured up, then went out and pitched.

Boy did he pitch.

With blood seeping from his ankle, which really did give him a red sock, Schilling gutted his way through seven innings, allowing one run and four hits while striking out four to pick up the 4-2 win. From the October

19th, 2004 espn.com article, Boston first baseman Kevin Millar said after the game, "When I saw that blood dripping through the sock and he's giving us seven innings in Yankee Stadium, that was storybook."

Millar's words couldn't be truer. Schilling's performance seemed to inspire his teammates in Game Seven, as they pounded the Yankees 10-3 to complete one of baseball's most remarkable comebacks. Down three games to none, the Red Sox won four straight to capture their first AL Pennant since 1986. That made the World Series almost anti-climactic, as the Bosox swept the Cardinals in four to finally break the 86-year-old Curse of the Bambino.

Schilling had another bloody sock outing in Game Two of the World Series, and again dominated the opposition, going six innings with a run, four hits and four strikeouts in a 6-2 win.

Injuries kept Schilling out of action for much of 2005. When he finally healed up in July, the Red Sox put him in the bullpen, where he saved nine games. He rebounded in 2006 with a 15-7 record, 3.97 ERA, 183 strikeouts and 28 walks in 204 innings of work. Schilling reached a milestone that year. On August 30th, he fanned Oakland's Nick Swisher for career strikeout 3,000.

Injuries dogged Schilling again in 2007. The 40-year-old righty went 9-8 with a 3.87 ERA. But he saved his best stuff for last. Schilling won three of his four post-season starts to help the Sox win their second World Series in three years.

He re-signed with Boston for 2008, but shoulder injuries kept him sidelined the entire season. Before the start of the 2009 campaign, Schilling officially announced his retirement, closing the book on one heck of a twenty-year career.

Since his retirement, Schilling has had his named bandied about as a candidate for political office, though he has not run for any. For a time, he ran his own video game company, which was forced to close not long after its creation. Schilling presently serves as an analyst on ESPN. While there is debate on whether Schilling belongs in the Hall of Fame, he was named by *Sports Illustrated* in 1999 as #11 on their list of Greatest Arizona Sports Figures.

He has also never shied away from expressing his opinion regarding various issues surrounding baseball. Though there was one time he resorted to actions instead of words. In 2003, Major League Baseball used a special camera called Questec to evaluate how umpires called balls and strikes. Schilling railed against the system, calling it "flawed" and saying that umpires told him they were changing their strike zones based on Questec's findings. After verbally expressing his displeasure, Schilling wrecked one of the Questec cameras during a game. Not only did he get his point across, he also got fined $15,000.

Career:
High School: Shadow Mountain (Phoenix), Class of 1985
College: Yavapai College (1986)
MLB: 1988-2007
Clubs: Baltimore Orioles (1988-1990); Houston Astros (1991); Philadelphia Phillies (1992-2000); Arizona Diamondbacks (2000-2003); Boston Red Sox (2004-2007)
Throws: Right
Bats: Right
Record: 216-146
Saves: 22
ERA: 3.46
Strikeouts: 3,116
Walks: 711
Shutouts: 20
Games: 569
Innings Pitched: 3,261
Complete Games: 83
League Leader Wins: 2001 (22), 2004 (21)
League Leader Strikeouts: 1997 (319), 1998 (300)
League Leader Complete Games: 1996 (8), 1998 (15), 2000 (8), 2001 (6)
League Leader Innings Pitched: 1998 (268), 2001 (256)
The Sporting News **NL Pitcher of the Year:** 2001, 2002
MLB All-Star: 1997, 1998, 1999, 2001, 2002, 2004
Post-Season Appearances: 1993, 2001, 2002, 2004, 2007
World Series Appearances: 1993, 2001, 2004, 2007
World Series Championships: 2001, 2004, 2007
Arizona Sports Hall of Fame: 2011

The number three man in the rotation, like Billy Hatcher, proves that not all Major League talent in Arizona comes from the Phoenix or Tucson metropolitan areas. He went from playing in a small mountain town to pitching on baseball's biggest stage.

That man is John Denny.

Hailing from Prescott, Denny was a strikeout machine his senior year. He racked up 116 with some very impressive single-game K totals. In one seven inning contest in 1969, he fanned 14 batters. Another time, the Prescott Badgers played a nine inning game in which Denny punched out 17. Finally, there was a ten inning game where he recorded 19 strikeouts. Denny finished his final year in high school with a 1.75 ERA and an All-State Honorable Mention.

Denny's coach at Prescott, Les Fenderson, called him, "A tremendous competitor," and added, "When I played at the UofA, I spent a lot of the time in the bullpen warming up various pitchers, and John, by the time he was a junior, threw the ball harder and more accurately than any of the pitchers we had on my UofA team, and of course, we came in second at the World Series."

In Denny's senior year, the scouts, according to Fenderson, "Came out of the woodwork. But he had sprained his ankle playing rec [basketball] and that inhibited a number of scouts in really being interested in him."

The scout for St. Louis, however, remained interested in him. Following graduation, the Cardinals drafted Denny, but not very high. He went in the 29th Round, 679th overall. He would ultimately be one of two players in that round to make it to the majors, the other being Bob Myrick, who pitched in 82 games for the New York Mets from 1976-1978, going 3-6 with two saves and a 3.48 ERA.

Denny spent his first year as a pro with the Gulf Coast League Cardinals in Florida. Splitting time between the starting rotation and the bullpen, the 17-year-old Prescottonian went 2-2 with a 1.29 ERA, two saves, one complete game, 43 strikeouts and nine walks in 42 innings of work. His next two seasons in Single-A, however, were ones of struggle. Between the St. Petersburg Cardinals and the Modesto Reds, Denny went a combined 15-18 with 142 strikeouts and 101 walks in 231 innings. In spite of those less-than-stellar numbers, he was promoted to AA in 1973. He turned his fortunes around with the Arkansas Travelers, going 10-6 with a 3.12 ERA, eight complete games, 81 strikeouts and 52 walks in 147 innings. He went up the ladder to AAA in 1974. While not earth shattering, his stats for the Tulsa Oilers were respectable. A 9-8 record with a 3.75 ERA, five complete games, two shutouts, 79 strikeouts and 57 walks in 132 innings.

After toiling for five years in the minors, Denny finally got his big break in when he was a September call-up for the St. Louis Cardinals. He immediately found himself in a pennant race as the Cards were chasing the Pittsburgh Pirates for first in the NL East. His contributions to that race were limited to just two appearances, both in relief, and both lasting one inning. Still, he gave up zero earned runs. In the end, the Cardinals missed out on the East crown by one-and-a-half games.

The next season, Denny made the big club out of spring training. But after starting 2-2, it was back to AAA. He quickly straightened himself out and was soon back in Cardinal red. Denny recalled in an October 10th, 2011 David Bromberg article on the website *Baseball Analysts*, "When I came back, I won seven games in a row. I'm 9-2 and some people were talking about me as a Rookie of the Year candidate. One day I'm jogging in the outfield in Cincinnati and I tore a lateral ligament."

Denny pitched through the injury and ended up 10-7 with a 3.97 ERA, three complete games, two shutouts, 72 strikeouts and 51 walks in 136 innings. He came back healthy in 1976, only to watch his Cardinals struggle. The team went 72-90 and finished 29 games out of first. Denny, however, went 11-9 and won the NL ERA title with a mark of 2.52 at the age of 23.

The next three seasons were up and down ones. Denny went 8-8 in 1977, then rebounded in 1978 with a 14-11 record, 2.96 ERA, 11 complete games, two shutouts and 103 strikeouts. He regressed in 1979, going 8-11 with a 4.85 ERA, 99 strikeouts and 100 walks. That December, his decade-long affiliation with the Cardinals organization came to an end. Denny was traded, along with outfielder Jerry Mumphrey, to the Cleveland Indians for Bobby Bonds. After going just 8-6 with a 4.39 ERA in 16 starts in 1980, Denny did better in the strike-shorted 1981 season, throwing three straight shutouts late in the year to finish 10-6 with 3.15 ERA, 94 strikeouts and 66 walks in 145 innings of work. Feeling they might have an emerging ace, the Indians signed Denny to a three-year, $2 million dollar contract, a fairly big deal back then.

Denny did not show ace stuff in 1982. He went 6-11 with a 5.01 ERA before the Tribe traded him late in the season to the Philadelphia Phillies for three players; Outfielder Wil Culmer, who played seven games in the majors, pitcher Jerry Reed, who went 20-19 with 18 saves in nine big league seasons, and pitcher Roy Smith, who went 30-31 in eight MLB seasons. Denny lost two of the four games he pitched for the Phils in the final month of the season. Most Philadelphia fans probably did not expect much from him in 1983.

But the hurler from "Everybody's Hometown" surprised them and everyone else in the baseball world with a career year. He led the National League with 19 wins and was second in ERA with a 2.37 mark. He also fanned a career-high 139 batters while completing seven games and throwing a career best 242 innings. Denny was the overwhelming choice for the NL Cy Young and even got a few votes for MVP, finishing 13th in that race. Along with all those regular season accomplishments, Denny did something he had not done in his previous nine seasons.

Pitch in the post-season.

Even with a roster that featured aging veterans like 38-year-old Steve Carlton, 39-year-old Joe Morgan, 40-year-old Ron Reed, 41-year-old Tony Perez and 42-year-old Pete Rose, the Phillies went 90-72 and won the NL East. Going into the NLCS, it appeared the odds were against them as they faced the Los Angeles Dodgers, who took 11 of 12 games from Philadelphia during the regular season.

The Phils, though, got the better of the Dodgers, with Carlton throwing a 1-0 shutout victory in the first game. Denny got the ball for Game Two. While he only allowed five hits and struck out three, his defense let him down. Errors in the first and fifth innings led to three Dodger runs. L.A. won the game 4-1.

The Phillies, however, took the next two games by identical scores of 7-2 to capture their second National League Pennant in four seasons. Denny would get to live the dream of everyone who ever picked up a ball and a mitt. He would play in the World Series.

Denny didn't wait long for his moment on baseball's biggest stage. Manager Paul Owens named him the starter for Game One versus the Baltimore Orioles.

The first inning did not go the way Denny would have liked. After getting leadoff man Al Bumbry to fly out, Jim Dwyer, a teammate of

Denny's in St. Louis, belted a solo home run. During an interview I conducted with Denny for my radio show, he recalled how he felt the ground under his feet shake from the raucous applause of 52,000 Orioles fans at old Memorial Stadium after Dwyer connected off him.

Instead of succumbing to it, Denny put the homer behind him and shut down the O's the rest of the way. He struck out five, walked none and gave up five hits through eight innings before Al Holland came in for the save as the Phillies won 2-1, those two runs coming off solo blasts by Garry Maddox and Joe Morgan.

That was the only victory for the Phils in the series. They dropped their next four games, with Denny taking the loss in Game Four, as the Orioles won their first World Championship since 1970.

1984, however, was an off-year for Denny. Arm problems put him on the disabled list. While he did have a 2.45 ERA, he went just 7-7. He put up an 11-14 record with a 3.82 ERA and 123 strikeouts in 1985 before the Phillies traded him and pitcher Jeff Gray to the Cincinnati Reds for reliever Tom Hume and outfielder Gary Redus. Denny didn't do too bad his one and only year in Cincy. He went 11-10 with a 4.20 ERA, two complete games, one shutout, 115 strikeouts and 56 walks in 171 innings. He was granted free agency after the 1986 season, but like Bob Horner, Denny, too, was a victim of collusion and had difficulty finding another team willing to sign him. That, and arm troubles, brought his career to an end at the age of 33.

In 13 big league seasons, Denny won ten or more games seven times and struck out 100 or more batters five times. To date, he is one of two pitchers with Arizona roots to win a Cy Young Award. Jim Palmer, as you read previously, being the other. In 1999, *Sports Illustrated* put Denny at #14 on their list of Arizona's Greatest Sports Figures. He also has a plaque hanging on the Hall of Fame wall at Prescott High School.

Coach Fenderson recalled one of Denny's earliest outings for the Cardinals when he went up against a future Hall of Famer.

"He was pitching against Johnny Bench, and when he went to throw the ball, it slipped out of his hand. Luckily, there was nobody on base, so there was no balk. Johnny Bench just cocked his head and was laughing at John, and John gave him that typical stare that was characteristic of him. Then the next pitch, he threw him a change up and broke {Bench's} bat, and it was hilarious. John broke into the biggest grin you ever saw in your life."

Denny learned a valuable lesson during his career, to always let Hall of Famer Lou Brock pick up the tab for lunch. In another radio interview I conducted with him, he related a story about his rookie year when Brock took him to lunch during a road trip in Montreal. When Denny went to pay for his meal, the Cardinal legend told him, "I got it."

Denny insisted on paying and pulled out a five dollar bill. Brock took it, ripped it in half, and said, "Kid, when I tell you I'm buying lunch, I'm buying lunch."

Career:
High School: Prescott, Class of 1969
MLB: 1974-1986
Clubs: St. Louis Cardinals (1974-1979); Cleveland Indians (1980-1982);
Philadelphia Phillies (1982-1985); Cincinnati Reds (1986)
Throws: Right
Bats: Right
Record: 123-108
ERA: 3.59
Strikeouts: 1,146
Walks: 778
Shutouts: 18
Games: 325
Innings Pitched: 2,148
Complete Games: 62
League Leader Wins: 1983 (19)
League Leader ERA: 1976 (2.52)
League Leader Assists by Pitcher: 1978 (73)
Cy Young Award: 1983
World Series Appearance: 1983

Some players have good seasons, others have great seasons. But few are part of miracle seasons. One of those is the fourth man in the Arizona All-Time Baseball Team's rotation, as he was part of the fabled 1969 Miracle Mets.

He is Gary Gentry.

Pitching, however, was not on Gentry's radar when he played for Camelback High School in Phoenix. His position was second base. But after showing off a powerful arm in the field, he felt the best way to continue his baseball career after graduation was on the mound.

That decision could not have worked out better for Gentry. After receiving his diploma in 1964, he signed with Phoenix College, the National Champions in 1960 and 1962. Thanks to Gentry, the Bears won another JUCO national title in 1965. That fostered a lot of interest from Major League teams, to the point he was drafted three times during his two years at Phoenix College. The Astros picked him in the 11th Round - 202nd overall - in the 1965 June Amateur Draft. Seven months later, the Orioles selected him in the First Round – seventh overall – in the January secondary draft. Six months later, it was the Giants who picked him in the Third Round, 41st overall.

Gentry did not sign with any of them. Instead, he opted to play for ASU in 1967. It was in Tempe where he not only rewrote the Western Athletic Conference record book, but also picked up another championship ring.

Gentry led the WAC with 19 wins, a conference record that would be tied by two other Sun Devils, Larry Gura in 1969 and Floyd Bannister in 1976. He also set the WAC record for most strikeouts in a season with 229 and most innings pitched in a single game, 15, versus ASU's arch-rival UofA in the WAC Southern Division playoff. He came close to tying that record in the College World Series, as he threw 14 innings in the Sun Devils 4-3 triumph over Stanford, a game where Gentry struck out 15 batters and scored the game-winning run. ASU beat Houston the next day 11-2 to capture the national title for the second time in team history.

Along with winning his second collegiate national championship, Gentry was named to the All College World Series Team and the NCAA All-American Team. The icing on the cake for those individual honors was the National College Player of the Year Award, making him the third straight Sun Devil to win it. The two before him? Rick Monday, who had a successful career for the Cubs and Dodgers, in 1965, and Mr. October himself, Hall of Famer Reggie Jackson, in 1966.

All of Gentry's accomplishments drew the interest of the New York Mets, who selected him in Round Three – 60th overall – in the 1967 MLB Draft. This time, he inked a pro contract. It should also be noted that two of Gentry's ASU teammates went in that same round, third baseman David Grangard (Twins, 43rd overall) and the College World Series' Most Outstanding Player, Ronald Davini (Yankees, 49th overall). Neither made it to the majors.

Gentry did, and it didn't take him long to do it.

The Mets were so impressed with him they didn't even bother starting him in Single A. He was assigned to the AA Williamsport Mets, going 4-4 with a 1.59 ERA, 77 strikeouts and 35 walks in 79 innings. The next season, Gentry pitched for the AAA Jacksonville Suns and experienced even more success. He put up a record of 12-8 with a 2.91 ERA, 156 strikeouts and 87 walks in 198 innings. When 1969 rolled around, Gentry came out of spring training as the number three starter for the New York Mets.

Not much was expected from this team. They were coming off a 73-89 season, which by Mets standards at the time wasn't too bad, when you consider they'd lost 100 or more games in five of their first seven seasons. But in 1969, instead of being cellar dwellers, they had a year some called "Amazin'," and others called a "Miracle."

The 22-year-old Gentry didn't do too bad in his first MLB season. He went 13-12 with a 3.43 ERA, three shutouts, six complete games, 154 strikeouts and 81 walks in 233 innings. The Mets rebounded from a sub-.500 start and gained ground on the first place Cubs, but were still nine-and-a-half games out of first in mid-August. Then in early September, the two clubs met for a critical series at Shea Stadium. In the September 9th contest, Cubs legend Ron Santo was in the on-deck circle when a black cat someone put on the field ran past him. The cat brought bad luck to Chicago as they lost the game 7-1 to extend their losing streak to six in a row. The Cubs lost their next two games, and after that, lost ten of their final 18 contests. The Mets, meanwhile, went on to win 18 of their final 23 games with Gentry going 3-1 during that stretch. In one of those games, September 24th, Gentry took on future Hall of Famer Steve Carlton, then with the Cardinals. The ex-Sun Devil tossed a complete game, four-hit shutout, striking out five in a 6-0 victory that clinched the National League Eastern Division for New York. That set the stage for the first ever National League Championship Series with the Mets taking on Hank Aaron, Phil Niekro, Orlando Cepeda and the rest of the Atlanta Braves.

The Hall of Fame talent of the Braves did not intimidate the Mets. They took the first two games of the series, and Gentry got the start for Game Three. He got off to a rough start, giving up a two-run homer to Aaron in the first inning. Gentry was relieved after two innings by none other than Nolan Ryan. The Mets came back to win 7-4 to sweep the Braves and move on to the World Series versus the Baltimore Orioles, who won 109 games and swept the Twins in the ALCS.

The series was tied 1-1 when Gentry got the ball for Game Three. His opponent, none other than the ace of Arizona's All-Time Baseball Team, Jim Palmer. In this battle of Grand Canyon State products, it was Gentry who came out on top. He threw six-and-two-thirds innings of shutout ball, striking out four, before being relieved, again, by Nolan Ryan. Not only that, but Gentry stroked a two-run double off Palmer in the second inning to give the Mets a 3-0 advantage. They went on to win 5-0, with Gentry getting the victory and Ryan the save. New York took the next two games to win the World Series and cement themselves forever as "The Miracle Mets."

For Gentry, it was his third championship in five seasons.

1970 was a so-so year for the Camelback High grad. He went 9-9 with a 3.68 ERA, 134 strikeouts and 86 walks in 188 innings. The next season it looked like Gentry got back on track. He posted a 12-11 record with a 3.23 ERA and career highs in strikeouts with 155, innings pitched with 203 and complete games with eight. 1972, however, saw him take a big step backwards. Gentry went 7-10 with a 4.01 ERA. Disappointed with his performance, but still feeling he had some value, the Mets traded Gentry and fellow pitcher Danny Frisella to the Braves for second baseman Felix Millan and pitcher George Stone.

Using the change of scenery to rejuvenate his career wasn't in the cards for Gentry. Bone chips in his elbow limited his playing time. In three seasons with the Braves, Gentry appeared in only 26 games, going 5-7 with a 3.57 ERA. He was released in May of 1975. The Mets decided to give him a second chance and assigned him to the AA Jackson Mets. He appeared in just one game, injuring his arm after a few pitches. A short time after, the Mets released Gentry, his baseball career over at the age of 28.

With his rocket arm and early success, Gentry is one of those "what if" players. What if he had stayed healthy? One of Gentry's teammates on the Miracle Mets, outfielder Ron Swoboda, said in Peter Golenbock's book *Amazin': The Miraculous History of New York's Most Beloved Baseball Team,* that the ex-Sun Devil's stuff was just as good as Seaver's.

Gentry returned to Arizona after retirement, where he managed subsidized housing units for senior citizens in Scottsdale. In 1976, he was inducted into the ASU Hall of Fame. Twenty-four years later, in 2010, he made it into another Hall of Fame, this one at Phoenix College.

During his career, Gentry wasn't only about throwing the ball. He fielded it just as well. In his seven-year major league career, he committed only *one* error in 182 chances for a .995 fielding percentage.

Career:
High School: Camelback (Phoenix), Class of 1964
College: Phoenix College (1965-1966); ASU (1967)
MLB: 1969-1975
Clubs: New York Mets (1969-1972); Atlanta Braves (1973-1975)
Throws: Right
Bats: Right
Record: 46-49
ERA: 3.56
Strikeouts: 615
Walks: 369
Shutouts: 8
Games: 157
Innings Pitched: 902
Complete Games: 25
Saves: 2
College Player of the Year: 1967
World Series Championship: 1969
ASU Hall of Fame: 1976
Phoenix College Hall of Fame: 2010

Rounding out the starting rotation is a man who spent the vast majority of his career in the bullpen, until he joined the Oakland A's at the dawn of Billy Beane's "Moneyball." That's where he had his most successful years as a pro.

He is Gil Heredia.

Growing up along the Mexican border, Heredia made the varsity baseball team at Nogales High School his freshman year of 1980. The next year he helped his team win the state championship. During his final two years for the Apaches, he garnered more and more interest from college coaches. Heredia, like many others on Arizona's All-Time Baseball Team, opted to go the community college route and signed with Pima College in Tucson. He spent his two years as an Aztec pitcher infuriating opposing batters, striking out 151 and winning 21 games. Drafted twice while at Pima, by the Pirates in 1984 and the Orioles in 1985, Heredia declined to sign, instead transferring to the UofA. It turned out to be a good decision on his part. Why?

Because the Wildcats won the 1986 College World Series.

"He was an outstanding pitcher," said former UofA Coach Jerry Kindall. "He won some huge games for us. He's a tremendous competitor. He simply wouldn't take no for an answer when he went to the mound, even when he didn't have his good stuff. He had a very good slider, he had a good curveball and a sinking fastball. When he put those all together and had good control, he was virtually unhittable. But there were days when he didn't have his best control and would give up some hits, but he just fought back to get the outs."

Heredia was a key part of the Wildcats third national championship. He won 16 games in 1986 and threw 165 innings, both single-season records until future Twins 20-game winner Scott Erickson broke them both in 1989. Heredia was also named to the All-American Third Team and the All-Pac 10 Team.

Kindall said, "Jim Wing, our pitching coach, had a great relationship with Gilbert. The two of them were a key ingredient in our winning the championship. Jim is a terrific pitching coach, and Gil had a willingness to abide by Jim's instruction and changes. We didn't have to change Gil a lot. He came to us as a pretty polished pitcher."

After that wildly successful season, his win total dropped to 10 in 1987 with 94 strikeouts and a 4.03 ERA. Still, he made the All-Pac 10 Team again and impressed the Giants so much they drafted him in the Ninth Round, 230th overall.

Heredia began his pro career in 1987 with the short-season Single A Everett Giants. His time with them didn't last long, just three games. But he did a heck of a job in those three games, going 2-0 with a 3.60 ERA and 14 strikeouts. That earned him a quick promotion to the full season Single A Fresno Giants, where he went 5-3 with a 2.90 ERA, 60 strikeouts and 23 walks in 80 innings.

1988 was also a good year for Heredia. Pitching for the Single A San Jose Giants, he went 13-12 with a 3.49 ERA, nine complete games, 121 strikeouts and 46 walks in 206 innings. After a stint with AA Shreveport, Heredia spent his next two seasons in his native state pitching for the Phoenix Giants. He went 9-7 with a 4.10 ERA in 1990. The next season, he improved his ERA to 2.82, but had a sub-.500 record at 9-11. Still, it didn't prevent the San Francisco Giants from giving him a September call-up.

Not that his Major League debut was anything spectacular.

With San Fran down 9-1 to St. Louis in the seventh, Heredia was brought out of the bullpen to finish the game. He gave up five runs on six hits, including homers to Ray Lankford and Felix Jose, as the Cards won 14-1. Heredia wound up pitching seven big league games in 1991, going 0-2 with a 3.82 ERA.

The next season, after going 2-3 with a 5.40 ERA in thirteen games, Heredia was sent down to the minors, then out of the country. In August of 1992, he was traded to the Montreal Expos for outfielder Brett Jenkins, who never played a single game in the majors.

Heredia became a pretty good reliever north of the border. In 1993, he went 4-2 with a 3.92 ERA, 40 strikeouts and 14 walks in 57 innings as the Expos tried, and failed, to catch the Philadelphia Phillies in the race for the NL East crown. In 1994, the Expos were baseball's best team, with Heredia playing a part in their success. In 36 relief appearances and three starts, the ex-Wildcat went 6-3 with a 3.46 ERA, 62 strikeouts and 13 walks in 75 innings. Montreal had the best record in baseball on August 11th at 74-40. Expos fans were excited at the prospect of the team's first post-season appearance since 1981. Some even picked them to win the whole thing. Heredia had a championship in high school and a championship in college. Would he add a Major League championship as well?

He wouldn't. No one would in 1994, because on August 12th, the players went on strike and the rest of the season was wiped out.

When baseball resumed in 1995, Heredia's stats tumbled. He went 5-6 with a 4.31 ERA. Following the season, he signed with the Texas Rangers and did even worse. He went 2-5 with a 5.89 ERA. Heredia was released after the season, then went back to Montreal. He spent all of 1997 in the minors, going 0-4 with a 4.70 ERA for the AAA Ottawa Lynx. Midway through the season, the Expos sent Heredia back to the U.S., trading him to the Cubs for minor leaguers Saul Bustos and Dave Jefferson. Assigned to the AAA Iowa Cubs, he started to turn his career around. Heredia went 4-2 with a 3.86 ERA, 30 strikeouts and nine walks in 46 innings. However, the Cubs didn't keep him around. Once again a free agent, Heredia signed with the Oakland A's and began the 1998 season with the AAA Edmonton Trappers. He continued to do well, splitting time as a starter and a reliever. Heredia went 10-8 with a 3.67 ERA, six complete games, a save, 99 strikeouts and 18 walks in 144 innings. On August 22nd, the Nogales native made his return to the majors with the Athletics.

And this return was a triumphant one.

Getting the start in Game One of a double-header with the Detroit Tigers, Heredia pitched six innings, allowing two runs while scattering eight hits and striking out four for a 7-2 win. He had another big game September 2nd in The Bronx. Heredia got the start against the eventual World Champion Yankees and David Cone, who won 20 games that season. He stifled the vaunted Yankee offense, pitching seven-and-two-thirds of shutout ball, allowing just five hits and zero walks while striking out five in a 2-0 victory.

The next season, Heredia was moved completely out of the bullpen and into the A's starting rotation. It turned out to be one of the team's best moves as he became one of their best pitchers. While his ERA was pretty high at 4.81, he led the staff with 13 wins and 200 innings pitched, while striking out 117 and walking 34. Oakland finished 2nd in the AL West with an 87-75 record.

Then came 2000, the year "Moneyball" finally paid off.

Part of a staff that included 20-game winner Tim Hudson, 15-game winner Kevin Appier and up-and-comers Mark Mulder and Barry Zito,

Heredia went 15-11 with a 4.12 ERA, two complete games, 101 strikeouts and 66 walks in 198 innings. Oakland went 91-70 to win the AL West. Their reward? Facing the New York Yankees in the ALDS.

And it was Heredia who got the start in Game One. Opposing him on the mound was none other than Roger Clemens.

After giving up back-to-back RBI doubles to Luis Sojo and Scott Brosius in the second inning, Heredia settled down and stymied the Yankee hitters. He threw six innings, allowing three runs on seven hits while striking out three before the A's bullpen held down the Bombers the rest of the way, giving Heredia the 5-3 win for the biggest highlight of his big league career.

Heredia came back to pitch the fifth and deciding game of the series. Unfortunately, it would be the biggest lowlight of his big league career. He gave up six runs and never made it out of the first inning as the Yankees went on to win 7-5 to take the ALDS en route to another World Championship.

The bad performance in that Game Five carried over to 2001. Heredia went 7-8 with a 5.58 ERA and was left off the post-season roster when the A's met the Yankees in the ALDS, and lost to them again in five games. He was granted free agency after the season, but at age 35 had a hard time catching on with another team.

It turned out 2001 would be Heredia's final season as a major league player.

He has remained active since the end of his big league days. In 2003, he was the pitching coach for the Nogales Charros of the independent Arizona-Mexico League. He has also served in that capacity in the Arizona Diamondbacks' farm system. Heredia also helped organize the Oropeza-Heredia Golf Tournament to help youth organizations and schools in the Nogales area. In 1994, he was inducted into the UofA Hall of Fame.

During his college days, Heredia didn't only play ball on the diamond. Coach Kindall said many times when the Wildcats were on the road, Heredia and some of his teammates could be found playing wiffle ball in the hotel parking lot.

Career:
High School: Nogales, Class of 1983
Colleges: Pima College (1984-1985); UofA (1986-1987)
MLB: 1991-1996, 1998-2001
Clubs: San Francisco Giants (1991-1992); Montreal Expos (1992-1995); Texas Rangers (1996); Oakland A's (1998-2001)
Throws: Right
Bats: Right
Record: 57-51
ERA: 4.46
Strikeouts: 547
Walks: 221
Games: 267

Innings Pitched: 954
Complete Games: 4
Saves: 4
UofA Hall of Fame: 1994

BULLPEN

Even Hall of Famers and All-Stars have off days on the mound. When Palmer, Schilling and the other starters don't have their best stuff, or if their pitch count gets way up there, it's time for the call to the bullpen. So who answers that call for Arizona's All-Time Baseball Team? Let's start with the middle and long relievers, who in a pinch can be emergency starters. First on the list is a righty who was born in New Jersey, then moved to Arizona.

It's Bob Milacki.

A Trenton native, Milacki wound up playing his high school baseball in Lake Havasu City. After a standout senior season in 1982, which included being named to the *Arizona Republic's* All-Arizona Baseball Team, he headed to Prescott to play for Yavapai College and Coach Rod Soesbe, who said of him, "He was a big, strong kid who threw such a heavy ball. He had a good, live arm and was a real good competitor."

His one season for the Roughriders was anything but standout. Milacki went 4-4 with a 5.54 ERA, 30 walks, 48 hits and 17 strikeouts in 39 innings. Despite those harsh-looking stats, Baltimore took him in the Second Round of the 1983 MLB Draft, 29th overall. Soesbe explained why the Orioles took such a chance on Milacki. "When you look at his body and his arm strength and the competitor that he was, he just had a great pitching body and a good arm. You can just project those guys that have that ability to move up another level and another level. I think the scouts projected him to be that kind of player."

Assigned to the Class A Hagerstown Suns, Milacki's first professional season was much better than his first and only collegiate season. He went 4-5 in 1984, but with a 3.36 ERA, 62 strikeouts and 48 walks in 77 innings.

Milacki had a couple of so-so seasons before he started living up to his potential. Despite a 4.46 ERA, he went 11-9 for the Charlotte O's in 1987 with 101 strikeouts and 66 walks in 148 innings. The next year was even better as his wins and strikeouts went up and his ERA went down.

Splitting time between Charlotte and the AAA Rochester Red Wings, Milacki went 15-9 with a 2.65 ERA, 132 K's and 77 walks in 214 innings. He also threw three shutouts and 12 complete games. That earned him a September call up, and he quickly impressed Baltimore. He pitched eight innings in his major league debut on September 18th, 1988, fanning four and allowing just one hit, along with four walks, to earn a 2-0 victory over the Detroit Tigers. Following that gem, the Orioles lost eight of their next nine games and were riding a four-game losing streak when Milacki took the mound against the New York Yankees on September 28th. He went the distance, striking out ten and giving up three hits as Baltimore won 2-0.

No surprise, in 1989 Milacki started the season on the Baltimore roster and played a key role in their turn-around. After finishing 1988 in the cellar with a 54-107 record, the Orioles went 87-75 and ended up second in the AL East. Milacki went 14-12 with a 3.74 ERA, 113 strikeouts and 88 walks in 243 innings. He also led the American League in games started with 36.

Milacki suffered a big setback in 1990 as he was sidelined almost half the season with a sore shoulder, going 5-8 with a 4.46 ERA. He bounced back fairly well in 1991. Splitting time as a starter and reliever, he went 10-9 with a 4.01 ERA, 108 strikeouts and 53 walks in 184 innings. He also threw three complete games, one shutout and took part in one of the rarest feats in baseball. On July 13th, Milacki got the start against the defending American League champion Oakland A's. He threw six innings, fanning three and walking three, before Mike Flanagan, Mark Williamson and Gregg Olson pitched the final three innings for a 2-0 no-hit victory. In a September 27th, 2011 *Baltimore Sun* article, Milacki said of that day, "It's a lot more special if you do it all yourself, but then you think, 'How many times does this happen in the big leagues?' Not many."

Milacki was right. In the entire history of Major League Baseball, there have been only eleven combined no-hitters. Three of them, including Milacki's, have involved pitchers with Arizona connections. Tom Wilhelmsen of Tucson was one of six Seattle Mariner hurlers to no-hit the Los Angeles Dodgers on June 8th, 2012. Two years later, on September 1st, 2014, Ken Giles, who pitched for Yavapai College, was one of four Philadelphia Phillies to no-hit the Atlanta Braves 7-0.

Milacki's career suffered another reversal in 1992. He went 5-7 with a 6.34 ERA and was demoted to AAA Rochester. At the end of the year, he was granted free agency. Milacki had short stints with the Cleveland Indians in 1993, the Kansas City Royals in 1994 – where he went 0-5 with a 6.14 ERA – and the Seattle Mariners in 1996. On September 21st of that year, Milacki pitched an effective ninth inning against the Oakland A's, striking out two as the M's won 9-2.

That was his last appearance in the majors.

After pitching in just six games for the Osaka Kintetsu Buffaloes of the Japan Pacific League in 1997, and going 0-2, Milacki attempted a comeback in 1998 with the New Orleans Zephyrs, the Houston Astros

AAA club. He gave a good accounting of himself, going 10-8 with a 3.84 ERA, 104 strikeouts and 51 walks in 189 innings. The Astros, however, didn't keep him around the next year. Milacki spent 1999 with the Pittsburgh Pirates AAA team in Nashville, where he put up a 6-8 record and a 4.86 ERA. The dawn of the 21st Century found Milacki pitching for the St. Paul Saints of the Independent Northern Central League, where he posted an 11-6 record with a 4.03 ERA. Following that season, the 35-year-old Milacki hung up his glove.

That was not the end of his baseball career. Milacki has spent much of his post-playing career as a minor league pitching coach. At the time of this book's publication, he served in that role for the Phillies Single-A team in Clearwater.

As of 2014, Milacki is the only graduate of Lake Havasu High School to ever play in the majors.

Career:
High School: Lake Havasu, Class of 1982
Colleges: Yavapai College (1983)
MLB: 1988-1994, 1996
Clubs: Baltimore Orioles (1988-1992); Cleveland Indians (1993); Kansas City Royals (1994), Seattle Mariners (1996)
Throws: Right
Bats: Right
Record: 39-47
ERA: 4.38
Strikeouts: 387
Walks: 301
Games: 143
Innings Pitched: 795
Complete Games: 8
Saves: 1
League Leader Games Started: 1989 (36)

The next long reliever/middle reliever/emergency starter is someone who might have made it to the big leagues a lot sooner had it not been for World War II. That's because he spent the war years in the U.S. Navy.

He's Alex Kellner.

Considered one of the best baseball players that ever came out of Tucson, Kellner threw four no-hitters for Amphitheater High School before making his professional debut in 1941 at the age of 16. In his first outing for the Tucson Cowboys of the Arizona-Texas League, he threw a ten-inning complete game victory against the El Paso Texans. In a February 10th, 1953 *Tucson Daily Citizen* article that looked back on the game, El Paso's pitcher, Dick Jerome, was so impressed with Kellner's performance he said the teen, "had the stuff to go all the way to the big leagues."

The words would be prophetic, but it would be sometime before Kellner got his shot at the bigs.

After going 11-7 with a 3.23 ERA for the Class C Muskogee Reds in 1942, Kellner joined the Navy. He spent nearly a year in the Pacific Theater on the destroyer *USS Callaghan* before being reassigned stateside for the remainder of the war. Discharged in 1946, Kellner resumed his baseball career in 1947 with the Birmingham Barons, the AA affiliate of the Philadelphia Athletics. While he had a high ERA of 4.96, he ended that season above .500 with an 11-9 record.

Kellner got called up to the A's in 1948, making his major league debut on April 29th against the Boston Red Sox. After starter Bill McCahan gave up 2-run bombs to Sam Mele and future Hall of Famer Ted Williams, legendary Athletics manager Connie Mack brought in Kellner to relieve him. He threw six innings, giving up three runs, four hits and two walks while striking out four, including Red Sox legend Johnny Pesky. The Athletics wound up losing 11-5.

Kellner pitched in thirteen games for Philadelphia that year, twelve out of the bullpen, and accumulated a horrendous 7.83 ERA. He went back to the minors, where he pitched very well for the Class A Savannah Indians. Kellner went 9-3 with a 2.73 ERA. The next season he found himself back in the majors.

And what a season he had. Kellner became the ace of the staff, going 20-12 with a 3.75 ERA, 94 strikeouts and 129 walks in 245 innings. He also had nineteen complete games, a save and earned a spot on the American League roster for the 1949 All-Star Game. He almost won the Rookie of the Year Award, but came in second in the voting behind the St. Louis Browns Roy Sievers, who batted .306 with 16 homers, 91 RBIs and 84 runs scored.

Following that incredible rookie season, Kellner suffered one heck of a sophomore slump. He went from a 20-game winner in 1949 to a 20-game *loser* in 1950. Kellner got back on track a bit over the next three seasons, as he won in double digits in 1951 (11), 1952 (12) and 1953 (11). He also lost in double digits those same three years, with 14 losses in 1951 and 1952 and 12 in 1953. After a dismal 1954 that saw him go 6-17 with a 5.39 ERA, the Athletics left Philadelphia for Kansas City. The change of scenery seemed to benefit Kellner. In the team's first season in the Midwest, he went 11-8 with a 4.20 ERA, 75 strikeouts and 60 walks in 162 innings. He also tossed six complete games and a career-high three shutouts. The next two seasons saw Kellner go a combined 13-9, but after a poor start to the 1958 season (0-2, 5.88 ERA), he was put on waivers and claimed by the Cincinnati Redlegs. As an aside, the team most of us know as the Cincinnati Reds was called the Redlegs throughout most of the 1950s since "Reds" was a word associated with Communism and this was the height of the Cold War with the Soviet Union.

Anyway, Kellner served as both a starter and reliever, and was effective for Cincinnati in both roles. He started seven games and came out of the pen for the other eleven, posting a record of 7-3 with a 2.30 ERA, 42 strikeouts, 20 walks, 82 innings pitched and four complete games. Shortly after the season, Kellner was part of a six-player deal as the Redlegs sent him, infielder – and future Milwaukee Brewers manager – Alex Grammas and first baseman George Crowe to the St. Louis Cardinals for outfielder Del Ennis, infielder – and future Red Sox manager – Eddie Kasko and pitcher Bob Mabe. Kellner pitched in just 12 games for the Cards in 1959, mainly as a reliever, and didn't do too bad, going 2-1 with a 3.16 ERA, nineteen strikeouts and ten walks in 37 innings. Midway through the season, however, Kellner decided to retire at the age of 34.

Kellner passed away in his native Tucson May 3rd, 1996 at the age of 71. Six years before his death, he was part of the inaugural class of the Pima County Sports Hall of Fame. In *Sports Illustrated's* list of Arizona's Top 50 Athletes, Kellner came in at #48.

Along with being a pretty fair Major League pitcher, Kellner also showed his prowess with the bat. He was a career .215 hitter, which is very good for a pitcher. Kellner also had 57 RBIs in twelve big league seasons, with ten "ribees" in both the 1949 and 1952 campaigns. He smacked four career home runs, three of them in 1957.

Alex was not the only Kellner to make a name for himself in baseball. His brother, Walt, was a star player at the UofA before joining Alex on the Philadelphia Athletics for the 1952 and 1953 seasons. Walt was also a 2002 inductee into the Pima County Sports Hall of Fame. Alex's nephew, Joe, pitched for the UofA when they won the 1980 National Championship.

Career:
High School: Amphitheater (Tucson), Class of 1941
MLB: 1948-1959
Clubs: Philadelphia/Kansas City Athletics (1948-1958); Cincinnati Redlegs (1958); St. Louis Cardinals (1959)
Throws: Left
Bats: Right
Record: 101-112
ERA: 4.41
Strikeouts: 816
Walks: 747
Games: 321
Innings Pitched: 1,849
Complete Games: 99
Saves: 5
MLB All-Star: 1949
Pima County Sports Hall of Fame: 1990

Now we come to the late inning guys, the ones who come in to lockdown the win. Quite a few pitchers from Arizona did well as closers or set-up men. So which ones get to do it for Arizona's All-Time Baseball Team?

The first short reliever is someone whose major league career might best be remembered for an incident involving a bat rather than anything he did on the mound. He is Lerrin LaGrow.

Following a standout baseball and basketball career at Glendale High School, LaGrow pitched for ASU. After a decent 1968 season where he went 5-0, he turned into one of the big guns in the Sun Devils' rotation in 1969. LaGrow posted 14 wins, had a consecutive scoreless innings streak of 29 and helped the Sun Devils win the College World Series. In their second game of the tournament, he stymied the UCLA offense as ASU pulled out a 2-1 win in extra innings. In his next start versus New York University, LaGrow not only fanned nine, he went 3-4 at the plate with two RBIs in a 4-1 victory.

After two seasons with Arizona State, LaGrow was 19-1 with a 1.97 ERA. That impressed the Detroit Tigers so much they selected him in the Sixth Round of the 1969 MLB Draft, 139th overall. Not only that, they skipped over A-ball with LaGrow and assigned him to the AA Montgomery Rebels.

His first year as a pro, however, turned out to be a cringe-worthy experience. While LaGrow did have a respectable 3.64 ERA, he went 2-10 in his 14 starts, striking out 59 while walking 40 in 84 innings.

In 1970, he experienced a sophomore rebound. Still with Montgomery, LaGrow went 11-4 with a 2.10 ERA, 11 complete games, 126 strikeouts and 49 walks in 146 innings. Those numbers earned him the Player of the Year Award from the Southern League and a call-up by the Tigers. The 22-year-old LaGrow stepped on a major league mound for the first time on July 28th, 1970. It wasn't a very long debut. LaGrow relieved Joe Niekro in the eighth inning He faced Paul Schaal of the Kansas City Royals, gave up a single, then was relieved by Fred Scherman. LaGrow pitched in nine more games that year, going 0-1 with a 7.30 ERA. He spent all of 1971 in AAA with the Toledo Mud Hens and struggled the entire season, going 2-6 with a 6.00 ERA.

LaGrow turned things around in 1972. Used as both a starter and reliever, he went 8-6 for the Mud Hens with a 2.43 ERA, 92 strikeouts and 59 walks in 115 innings. The Tigers recalled him for their stretch run as they battled the Red Sox, Orioles and Yankees for the AL East crown. The Glendale grad turned out to be one of Detroit's most effective relievers during the last two months of the season. He posted two saves and a 1.32 ERA in 16 games as the Tigers won the division, beating out Boston by just half-a-game. At age 23, and with only 26 big league games under his belt, LaGrow was headed to the playoffs, where the Tigers faced the Oakland A's. He would make an appearance in the ALCS, and it would be a very brief one.

After dropping Game One 3-2 in 11 innings, Detroit found themselves down 5-0 after five innings in Game Two. LaGrow came out of the bullpen in the sixth inning and set down the A's in order. After the Tigers went down in order in the top of the seventh, LaGrow came back to pitch the bottom of the frame. What followed is the incident he is probably most remembered for as a major league pitcher.

Leading off for the A's was their famed shortstop Bert Campaneris, who had given the Tigers fits that day by going 3-3 with two runs scored and two stolen bases. He had also been brushed back on a previous trip to the plate, which possibly set the stage for what followed.

LaGrow uncorked a pitch that hit Campaneris in the ankle. When Campy got to his feet, he hurled his bat at LaGrow. The bat, fortunately, missed him. Campaneris was tossed from the game and suspended for the remainder of the ALCS.

So was LaGrow.

That turned out to be the only post season appearance of his career.

LaGrow scuffled over the next three seasons for the Tigers, mainly as a starter. From 1973-1975, he never had an ERA under 4.00, while losing 19 games in 1974 and 14 in 1975. He was let go by Detroit prior to the start of the 1976 season and picked up by St. Louis. The Cardinals assigned him to their AA affiliate, the Tulsa Oilers. He went 6-10 with a 4.14 ERA, six complete games, 108 strikeouts and 45 walks in 161 innings. Despite those numbers, LaGrow earned a September call-up and did a decent job as both a starter and a reliever, ending up with a 1.48 ERA in eight games.

After the season, LaGrow was on the move again. The Cardinals traded him to the Chicago White Sox for Clay Carroll, who had been an All-Star reliever for Cincinnati's "Big Red Machine" throughout much of the 1970s. It was in the Windy City that LaGrow experienced the most success of his big league career.

Manager Bob Lemon used LaGrow exclusively as a reliever, and he flourished in that role. He posted 25 saves in 1977, the third most in the American League, along with a 7-3 record, 2.46 ERA, 63 strikeouts and 35 walks in 98 innings. That helped the White Sox finish 90-72, a darn good record by any account. But not as good as the Kansas City Royals, who won the AL West with a 102-60 mark.

1978 was a decent year for LaGrow, too. While his ERA ballooned to 4.40, he did go 6-5 with 16 saves, 41 strikeouts and 38 walks in 88 innings. Teamwise, Chicago did a reversal from the year before, ending up 71-90 with Lemon fired in mid-season . . . then hired by the Yankees, who went on to win the World Series.

1979 started off as poorly as you can imagine for LaGrow. In eleven games, he was 0-3 with just one save and a stratospheric 9.17 ERA. The White Sox let him go little over a month into the season. He was purchased by the Los Angeles Dodgers and had a bit of a resurgence on the West Coast. LaGrow went 5-1 with four saves, a 3.41 ERA, 22 strikeouts and 18 walks in 37 innings. Following the season, LaGrow was granted free agency and headed to the opposite end of the country as he signed with the Phillies. There was a period from mid-June to early July of 1980 when he did fairly well. He had three saves, one of which halted a four-game losing streak for Philly. Unfortunately, it wasn't enough to keep him on the roster. With an 0-2 record and a 4.15 ERA in 25 games, Philadelphia released him in mid-July. The Phillies went on to win their first World Series, while LaGrow went into retirement at age 31.

Nine years after he threw his final pitch in the majors, LaGrow was honored by his alma mater as part of the 1989 induction class to the ASU Hall of Fame.

Career:
High School: Glendale, Class of 1967
College: ASU (1968-1969)
MLB: 1970, 1972-1980
Clubs: Detroit Tigers (1970, 1972-1975); St. Louis Cardinals (1976); Chicago White Sox (1977-1979); Los Angeles Dodgers (1979); Philadelphia Phillies (1980)
Throws: Right
Bats: Right
Record: 34-55
Saves: 54
ERA: 4.11
Strikeouts: 375
Walks: 312
Games: 309
Innings Pitched: 779
Complete Games: 19
Post-Season Appearance: 1972
ASU Hall of Fame: 1989

Now we come to our lefty setup man, who didn't look like anything special early in his career. Later on, however, he became an important cog for not one, not two, but three world championship teams.

He's Jeremy Affeldt.

While this book has featured several players who were born in other states before moving to Arizona, Affeldt breaks that trend. Born in Phoenix in 1979, Affeldt didn't stay there long. In fact, he didn't stay in many places for long. With his father serving in the Air Force, Affeldt moved from Arizona to Guam, then to California. When his father retired, the family settled in Colbert, Washington, a small town near Spokane. How small was it? When Affeldt received his diploma from Northwest Christian High School in 1997, his graduating class consisted of nineteen seniors.

After a phenomenal high school career, Affeldt was drafted by the Kansas City Royals in the Third Round, 91st overall. They assigned him to the Gulf Coast League Royals, where he went 2-0 with 36 strikeouts in 40 innings. On the flip side, he walked 21 batters and had a 4.50 ERA.

Affeldt's time in the minors was marked by a series of ups and downs. One up came in 1999 with the Single A Charlestown Alleycats. He went 7-7 with a 3.83 ERA while striking out 111. One down came the next season. Promoted to the advanced Single A Wilmington Blue Rocks, Affeldt went 5-15 with a 4.09 ERA. Despite those numbers, the Royals moved him up to AA in 2001. He rebounded with the Wichita Wranglers, going 10-6 with a 3.90 ERA, 128 strikeouts and 48 walks in 145 innings.

The next stop for Affeldt was not AAA. With the Royals not having a winning season in seven years, the higher ups felt they had nothing to lose by bringing Affeldt straight to the majors. He made his MLB debut on April 6th, 2002. Already down 8-0 to the White Sox in the fifth inning, Affeldt came out of the bullpen and threw a scoreless sixth inning. In the seventh, he gave up a leadoff double to All-Time Arizona teammate Paul Konerko, who eventually scored on a Sandy Alomar, Jr. single. Affeldt was replaced after that inning, and the Royals ultimately lost 14-0.

Oh by the way, Affeldt's battery mate that day was A.J. Hinch, the Diamondbacks manager from 2009-2010.

Affeldt ended his rookie year with a 3-4 record, a 4.64 ERA, 67 strikeouts and 37 walks in 77 innings. The next season went a little better as his ERA dropped to 3.93, his strikeouts increased to 98 and he ended up with a 7-6 record. In 2004, he was tabbed as the Royals closer, saving 13 games, but accumulating a 4.95 ERA. That earned run average went even higher in 2005, to 5.26. Midway through the 2006 season, Affeldt and pitcher Denny Bautista were traded to the Colorado Rockies for reliever Scott Dohmann and first baseman Ryan Shealy. Between the two teams, Affeldt's ERA was a combined 6.20.

In 2007, he halted the trend of his ERA climbing into the stratosphere. He turned into an effective late inning man for the Rockies, going 4-3 and cutting his ERA almost in half to 3.51. Affeldt also fanned 46 and walked 33 in 59 innings. Colorado won the NL Wildcard with a 90-73 record, giving Affeldt his first taste of post-season play.

His playoff debut, however, got off to a shaky start.

Brought in for the sixth inning of Game Two of the National League Divisional Series versus the Philadelphia Phillies, Affeldt gave up a leadoff home run to Ryan Howard. He settled down and retired the next three batters as the Rockies won the game 10-5 and went on to sweep the series.

Affeldt was dominating for the rest of the post-season. He allowed no runs, hits or walks in two appearances in the NLCS against the Arizona Diamondbacks. Colorado won the series in four games and met the Red Sox in the World Series. Even though they were swept by Boston, Affeldt turned in a good performance in the Fall Classic. He saw action in all four games, giving up no runs and two hits while striking out two.

After the season, Affeldt tested the free agent market and signed with the Cincinnati Reds. He put together a good season, going 1-1 with a 3.33 ERA, 80 strikeouts and 25 walks in 78 innings.

Affeldt was on the move again in 2009, signing with the San Francisco Giants. It was in the city by the bay that he experienced the most success in his baseball career.

In his first season with the Giants, Affeldt went 2-2 with a 1.73 ERA, 55 strikeouts and 31 walks in 62 innings. He was also named the Setup Man of the Year. His second season, however, saw him take a step back. Affeldt's ERA ballooned to 4.14. Those struggles continued into the post-season, as he had ERAs of 3.38 in the NLCS and 6.75 in the World Series. Still, the Giants rolled over the Texas Rangers, winning the series in five games and earning Affeldt his first championship ring.

He got back on track in 2011, going 3-2 with a 2.63 ERA, three saves, 54 strikeouts and 24 walks in 61 innings. The next season he posted a 1-2 record with a 2.70 ERA, three saves, 57 strikeouts and 23 walks in 63 innings as San Francisco returned to the post-season. That's where Affeldt shined. In ten appearances, he did not allow a single run while giving up five hits and striking out ten. Perhaps his biggest moment came in Game Four of the World Series versus the Detroit Tigers. Replacing starter Matt Cain in the eighth and with the score tied 3-3, Affeldt walked Avisail Garcia to start the inning, then fanned MVP and Triple Crown winner Miguel Cabrera, All-Star slugger Prince Fielder and Delmon Young. San Francisco won the game 4-3 in ten innings to sweep the Tigers, giving Affeldt his second World Series ring.

Limited to 39 games in 2013 due to injuries, Affeldt rebounded with a successful 2014 campaign, going 4-2 with a 2.28 ERA, 41 strikeouts and a career-low 14 walks in 55 innings. His contributions out of the pen helped the Giants get back to the post-season. He pitched three games in the NLDS, holding the Washington Nationals scoreless as San Francisco took the series 3-1. Next, the Giants met the Cardinals in the NLCS. In Game Five, Affeldt entered the ninth inning with the bases loaded and two outs and the scored knotted at three. He got Oscar Taveras to ground out to end the inning, setting the stage for Travis Ishikawa's walk-off three-run homer to end the series and send the Giants back to the World Series. Their opponent, Affeldt's former team, Kansas City.

He pitched more shutout ball in Games Two, Three and Four. In Game Seven, Affeldt was called on in the second inning to replace the struggling Tim Hudson. He pitched shutout ball through the fourth inning before being relieved by Madison Bumgarner. The Giants held off a late Royals rally to win 3-2, capturing their third World Series title in five seasons. Affeldt was credited with the victory, giving him a 2-0 record and a 0.00 ERA for the post-season.

To show that Affeldt did not forget his roots, when he initially signed with the Kansas City Royals, he donated the money from his signing bonus to his old high school in order for them to build a new baseball field.

Career (as of 2014):
High School: Northwest Christian (Colbert, WA), Class of 1997
MLB: 2002-present
Clubs: Kansas City Royals (2002-2006); Colorado Rockies (2006-2007);
Cincinnati Reds (2008); San Francisco Giants (2009-present)
Throws: Left
Bats: Left
Record: 41-44
ERA: 3.89
Saves: 28
Strikeouts: 699
Walks: 382
Games: 722
Innings Pitched: 890
MLB Setup Man of the Year: 2009
Post-Season Appearances: 2007, 2010, 2012, 2014
World Series Appearances: 2007, 2010, 2012, 2014
World Series Championships: 2010, 2012, 2104

The right-handed set up man is someone who did well in that role throughout a good portion of his thirteen-year big league career. He is also someone who won a championship ring before he signed his first pro contract.

He's Bobby Howry.

Born in Phoenix, Howry was a standout player at Deer Valley High School, not that he started out that way. His coach at the time, Mike Cornish, said, "I thought of his freshman year. He was a pretty tall and skinny kid, and had a hard time finding the backstop behind the catcher. But as he progressed, he started to fill out. He really got dedicated in the weight room. By the time he got to his senior year, he was a solid 6'5 and I think 225, and the scouts were out in droves."

After graduation, Howry headed north to Prescott to play for Yavapai College. His first year in a Roughrider uniform was less-than-stellar. Howry went 5-6 with a 5.81 ERA in 1992. Still, the Houston Astros selected him in that year's draft in the 29th Round, 797th overall. He elected to return to Yavapai for his sophomore season.

It turned out not only Howry, but the entire team, benefited from that decision.

Howry became the ace of the Roughrider staff, helping them get to the Junior College World Series in Grand Junction, Colorado. There he won two games and Yavapai won the whole thing. Fresh off that memorable 1993 season, Howry was drafted again, and would you believe, much lower than after his sub-.500 1992 season. The expansion Florida Marlins picked him in the 45th Round, 1,269th overall. Instead of going pro, Howry continued his college career with McNeese State in Lake Charles, Louisiana. Following his 1994 season, Howry was drafted again, but much, much higher. The San Francisco Giants chose him in the Fifth Round, 144th overall. This time, he did sign.

His first pro season was one of struggle. Splitting 14 games between the Everett Giants and the Clinton Lumberkings, Howry went 1-7 with a five-dollar ERA. He rebounded in 1995 with the Single A San Jose Giants, going 12-10 with a 3.54 ERA, 107 strikeouts and 54 walks in 165 innings. He also posted an above .500 record the following season with the AA Shreveport Captains, going 10-8, but with a 4.65 ERA.

Howry remained in Shreveport in 1997, though instead of starting he became a closer. In spite of a 4.91 ERA, he went 6-3 with 22 saves, 43 strikeouts and 21 walks in 55 innings. Then on July 31st, he left Shreveport. In fact, he left the Giants organization all together.

Over in the American League, the Chicago White Sox were chasing the Cleveland Indians for the Central Division crown. Despite being only a handful of games out of first place, Sox General Manager Ron Schueler pulled the trigger on what became known as "The White Flag Trade." He sent closer Roberto Hernandez and starting pitchers Wilson Alverez and Danny Darwin to San Francisco for six prospects.

Howry was one of them.

He was assigned to the AA Birmingham Barons and fared well. In twelve games he had two saves and a 2.84 ERA. He earned a promotion to the AAA Calgary Cannons in 1998, saving five games with a 3.41 ERA, 22 strikeouts and ten walks in 31 innings. Then in June, Howry got the promotion he'd been waiting for, the one to The Show.

The Deer Valley grad made his major league debut on June 21st, 1998 as the White Sox took on the Minnesota Twins. When starter Jason Bere made an early exit after giving up six runs in four innings, Howry relieved him and shut out the Twins in the fifth and sixth innings. The Chicago offense, however, could do almost nothing against Minnesota starter Mike Morgan – who would be part of the Diamondbacks 2001 World Championship team – and lost 6-1.

Howry impressed the White Sox through the second half of the season, to the point he was closing most of their games in September. He ended his rookie season at 0-3 with nine saves, a 3.15 ERA, 51 strikeouts and 19 walks in 54 innings.

Over the next four seasons, Howry was used in both the closer and set-up roles, racking up 40 saves, with a career-high 28 in 1999. In 2000, he went 2-4 with a 3.17 ERA, seven saves, 60 strikeouts and 29 walks in 71 innings to help Chicago capture the AL Central title. Howry appeared in two games in the ALDS versus Seattle, giving up two hits, two walks and a run while striking out four in just under three innings of work. The Sox, however, were swept by Seattle.

In 2002, Howry was involved in another trade deadline deal as the White Sox sent him to the other Sox team in Boston for a pair of minor leaguers. His time with the Bosox was short and not enjoyable. After going 1-3 with a 5.00 ERA in the final two months of the season, the bottom dropped out for Howry in 2003. He had a 12.64 ERA in just four games and was demoted to AAA Pawtucket. Boston released him at the conclusion of the season.

Howry found a new home in Cleveland, and it rejuvenated his career. In two seasons with the Indians, he went 11-6 with a 2.57 ERA, three saves, 87 strikeouts and 28 walks in 115 innings. After the 2005 season, he opted for free agency and returned to Chicago, signing a three-year, $12 million dollar deal with the Cubs. His first two seasons with them were pretty consistent. He went 4-5 with a 3.17 ERA, five saves, 71 strikeouts and 17 walks in 76 innings in 2006, then posted a 6-7 record with a 3.32 ERA, eight saves, 72 strikeouts and 19 walks in 81 innings in 2007. That year the Cubs won the NL Central, and Howry made his second trip to the post-season. This time, he faced his hometown team, the Arizona Diamondbacks, in the divisional series. Howry performed well, getting in two games and pitching three shutout innings, allowing one hit and no walks while striking out six. Chicago as a whole, however, did not perform well, and were swept by the D-backs.

Howry spent one more year with the Cubs. While he did go 7-5 in 2008, his ERA skyrocketed to 5.35 and his strikeouts went down to 59. He also gave up a career high 13 homers. Granted free agency, he joined the team he originally signed with, the Giants. His ERA dropped to 3.39 in 2009, but he compiled a record of 2-6. The next season he went back home to join the D-backs, but it was not a fun homecoming. Howry pitched in 14 games and had a 10.67 ERA. He was released less than two months into the season, then picked up by the Cubs. Howry struggled with them as well, and was again released. Failing to catch on with another team, he officially retired before the start of the 2011 season, ending a thirteen-year big league career. It was a career that saw Howry end up on a pair of interesting lists. As of 2014, he is one of 174 players to have spent time with both the Chicago Cubs and White Sox. He is also one of eight Arizona-born players to have suited up for the Diamondbacks.

While Howry made his living as a pitcher, Coach Cornish said he was also one heck of a hitter in high school. "At Deer Valley, right field is 330 feet with an eight-foot fence. Then there's a roadway of about thirty feet up to our V-tech building, which must be twenty-five, maybe thirty feet high. Bobby hit a home run that landed on the middle of the building next to the refrigeration unit up on top."

Up until that point, the longest home run Cornish said he saw was hit by another member of Arizona's All-Time Baseball Team, Tim Salmon, during his time at Greenway.

If there was one aspect of conditioning Howry hated, it was running, as Cornish recalled, "He wasn't much into running. You wanted to punish him, you tell him to run ninety feet, and he'd be scared to death of that ninety feet."

Career:
High School: Deer Valley (Glendale), Class of 1991
Colleges: Yavapai College (1992-1993); McNeese State (1994)
MLB: 1998-2010
Clubs: Chicago White Sox (1998-2002); Boston Red Sox (2002-2003); Cleveland Indians (2004-2005); Chicago Cubs (2006-2008, 2010); San Francisco Giants (2009); Arizona Diamondbacks (2010)
Throws: Right
Bats: Left
Record: 45-52
Saves: 66
ERA: 3.84
Strikeouts: 653
Walks: 253
Games: 769
Innings Pitched: 787
Post-Season Appearances: 2000, 2007

Finally, we come to the man who shuts the door on games. The closer. Who is it who saves the day for Arizona's All-Time Baseball Team? It's a man with the first name of Robert and the unique middle name of Meiklejohn.

Most fans know him as Mike MacDougal.

Born in Las Vegas, MacDougal and his family moved to Mesa, where he excelled on the mound at Mesa High School. In his senior season, he put up a 9-2 record with an astounding 1.00 ERA. After graduation, the Baltimore Orioles selected him in the 22nd Round, 651st overall, but he declined to sign in favor of playing for Wake Forest University. It didn't take him long to make an impact at the collegiate level. Despite an ERA of 4.12, he went 6-4 his first year with the Demon Deacons with two saves, 85 strikeouts and 38 walks in 91 innings. That earned him a spot on the NCAA All-American Freshman Team.

While his freshman season was pretty good, MacDougal's junior season was outstanding. He went 13-3 with a 2.63 ERA, an ACC-best 117 strikeouts and 65 walks in 120 innings. He made the All ACC Team, the NCAA All-American First Team, and pitched Wake Forest's first no-hitter in 60 years. That resume wowed the Kansas City Royals so much they selected him in the First Round of the 1999 MLB Draft, 25th overall. MacDougal skipped his senior season and went pro.

Assigned to the Class-A Spokane Indians, he put up a high ERA of 4.47, but did fan 57 batters in 46 innings. The next season went better for MacDougal. Pitching for the Class A Wilmington Blue Rocks, he went 9-7 with a 3.92 ERA, one save, 129 strikeouts and 76 walks in 144 innings. In 2001, he made the jump to AAA, where he was 8-8 for the Omaha Golden Spikes with a 4.68 ERA, 110 strikeouts and 76 walks in 144 innings. When the Kansas City Royals made their September call-ups, MacDougal was part of that group. He made his major league debut on September 22nd, when KC gave him the start against the Chicago White Sox.

It was not the best of debuts.

MacDougal didn't get past the fifth inning, allowing three runs and six hits while striking out one. He wasn't involved in the decision, as the Royals came back to tie the game, only to lose it in the tenth on a Tony Graffanino sac fly, final score 5-4. Of note, the Royals tied the game in the eighth inning on an RBI double by Brent Mayne off none other than the set-up man for Arizona's All-Time Baseball Team, Bobby Howry.

After another season in the minors, and another cup of coffee with the Royals, in 2002, MacDougal made the big club full time in 2003. His role changed from starter to reliever, and he excelled at it. While he did have an ERA of 4.08 and a record of 3-5, MacDougal nailed down 27 saves, while striking out 57 and walking 32 in 64 innings of work. He was also named to the American League All-Star Team, though he did not get into the game.

2004, however, was anything but an All-Star season for MacDougal. An illness he suffered during the spring, coupled with a sore shoulder, limited him to thirteen games. He bounced back in 2005 with 21 saves, a 3.33 ERA, 72 strikeouts and 24 walks in 70 innings for a Kansas City team that lost 106 games. In 2006, MacDougal spent much of his time as a set up man, posting a 1.80 ERA with 19 strikeouts in 25 innings. Despite that performance, the Royals traded him to the White Sox for minor league pitchers Tyler Lumsden and Dan Cortes. After a horrific 2007 that saw MacDougal go on the DL, and post a 6.80 ERA at AAA Charlotte, he rebounded in 2008, dropping his ERA to 2.12 in sixteen games with Chicago. The rest of the year he spent in Charlotte. After a poor start to the 2009 season, the White Sox released MacDougal.

He wasn't out of work for long. In early May, he joined the Washington Nationals, who returned him to the role he was known for during his Kansas City days, closer.

MacDougal saved 20 games for the Nats in 2009 with an ERA of 3.60, though his 31 walks in 50 innings was cause for concern. He spent much of 2010 bouncing around the minors, then was signed by the Los Angeles Dodgers in 2011. MacDougal did well for them in middle relief, going 3-1 with a 2.05 ERA, one save, 41 strikeouts and 29 walks in 57 innings. That success didn't carry over to 2012. He had a 7.94 ERA in seven games and was released. Since that time, MacDougal has been with the Chicago Cubs, Washington Nationals (again), Cincinnati Reds, Philadelphia Phillies and Seattle Mariners organizations trying to get back to the big leagues. Following his release by Seattle in June of 2014, MacDougal wound up with the Camden Riversharks of the independent Atlantic League.

MacDougal's high school accomplishments earned him an induction into the Mesa City Sports Hall of Fame in 2009. For what he did at Wake Forest, he was inducted into their Hall of Fame in 2014.

Career:
High School: Mesa, Class of 1996
Colleges: Wake Forest University (1997-1999)
MLB: 2001-2012
Clubs: Kansas City Royals (2001-2006); Chicago White Sox (2006-2009); Washington Nationals (2009); St. Louis Cardinals (2010); Los Angeles Dodgers (2011-2012)
Throws: Right
Bats: Both
Record: 18-23
Saves: 71
ERA: 4.00
Strikeouts: 325
Walks: 212
Games: 407
Innings Pitched: 394
MLB All-Star: 2003
Mesa City Sports Hall of Fame: 2009
Wake Forest University Hall of Fame: 2014

THE BENCH

Any good team needs a good bench to deliver clutch pinch hits or give the starters a day off. So who are the reserves that fill out the final seven roster spots for Arizona's All-Time Baseball Team?

The first one is the man who has the distinction of being, to date, Northern Arizona University's only contribution to the majors. He's George Grantham.

Born in Galena, Kansas at the turn of the 20th Century, Grantham and his family moved first to Flagstaff, then to Kingman. At age fifteen, Grantham attended Northern Arizona Normal School – now known as Northern Arizona University – where he played for their fledgling baseball team. World War I put his baseball career on hold as he lied about his age in order to join the U.S. Navy. Grantham served aboard a submarine that spent much of the war patrolling the waters off Cuba.

Shortly after the end of the so-called "War to End All Wars," Grantham returned to the states, where he signed his first pro contract in 1920 with the Tacoma Tigers of the Pacific Coast International League. He moved on to the Portland Beavers of the Pacific Coast League in 1921, batting .305 for them. The next season he played for the Omaha Buffaloes of the Western League and hit .359. In September of 1922, the Chicago Cubs purchased Grantham's contract. Not long after, on the 22nd of that month, he made his major league debut. He had a single, a run and stole a base as the Cubs got clipped by the Philadelphia Phillies 9-8.

The next season, Grantham made the Cubs roster out of spring training as their starting second baseman. He had an impressive .281 batting average, 70 RBIs, 43 stolen bases and 81 runs scored. Other stats, however, were less than impressive. Grantham led the National League in strikeouts with 92. Things were even more nightmarish in the field. In 150 games at second base, he committed 55 errors.

In 1924, Grantham upped his average to .316 and his strikeouts dropped to 63. He also reduced his number of errors . . . to 44.

Shortly after the season, Grantham was part of one of the most controversial trades of the 1920s. The Cubs sent him to the Pittsburgh Pirates, along with 15-game winner Vic Aldridge and minor leaguer Al Niehaus, in exchange for 20-game winner Wilbur Cooper, first baseman Charlie Grimm and future Hall of Fame infielder Rabbit Maranville. That trade outraged the Pirate faithful.

What Grantham did in 1925, however, quelled that outrage. He batted .326 with eight home runs, 52 RBIs, 74 runs scored, 24 doubles and 14 stolen bases. He also struck out just 29 times while drawing 50 walks and committing only eleven errors at his new position, first base. Thanks to Grantham's contributions, the Pirates went 95-58 and won the NL Pennant by eight-and-a-half games over the New York Giants.

Grantham had a very good World Series against the defending World Champions, the Washington Senators, at least defensively. He committed zero errors in 47 chances. Offensively, however, was another story. He had only two hits and one stolen base. His lack of production didn't hurt the Bucs in the end. They came back from being down three games to one to win the series. At age 25, Grantham was part of a world championship team.

The next season was also successful for him. He batted .318 with eight homers, 70 RBIs, 66 runs scored, 27 doubles and 13 triples. The Pirates, however, fell short of another pennant, finishing in third place, four-and-a-half games in back of the St. Louis Cardinals, who went on to beat the Yankees in seven games in the World Series.

In 1927, Pittsburgh returned to the Fall Classic, and Grantham again had a big hand in that. He batted .305 with eight home runs, 66 RBIs, 96 runs scored, 33 doubles, eleven triples and 74 walks. The Pirates survived a tight race for first, going 94-60 and beating out the Cardinals by one-and-a-half games. In the World Series, they faced the Yankees, winners of 110 games that year. Unlike in 1925, Grantham performed well at the plate, hitting .364. The Pirates, however, were no match for the famed "Murderers Row" led by future Hall of Famers Babe Ruth, Lou Gehrig and Tony Lazzeri. New York swept Pittsburgh in four straight.

Grantham spent four more seasons with the Pirates, hitting .300 or better each year. In 1930, he established career highs in home runs (18), RBIs (99) and runs scored (120) while batting .324. Prior to the start of the 1932 season, Grantham was sold to the Cincinnati Reds. He had a good season for them, batting .292 with 81 runs. The next season, however, his numbers tumbled. Appearing in 87 games, Grantham hit just .204. After the 1933 season, he was traded to the Giants for pitcher Glenn Spencer. He again struggled at the plate, hitting .241 in 32 games before being let go. Grantham spent 1935 with the Seattle Indians of the Pacific Coast League. Despite batting .286, no major league teams showed interest in him. He retired after that season.

Grantham returned to Kingman, where he worked as a manager at the Central Commercial Company until he passed away in 1954 at the age of 53.

Along with winning a World Series, another special day for Grantham occurred on April 1st, 1924. According to the *Daily Miner* newspaper, the Cubs and the Pirates played an exhibition game in Kingman. What the paper called "Kingman's Greatest Crowd" turned out to see Grantham's homecoming. According to one account written in the *Miner,* "George came through in fine shape, exceeding what might have been expected of him under the circumstances. Here he was back among his friends playing ball for the first time since he started his ascent to the big leagues. His mother was watching the game from the grandstand. George wanted to make good to the extent without doubt of being over anxious and thus at a disadvantage."

Grantham's current team, the Cubs, pounded his future team, the Pirates, 17-3.

Career:
High School: Flagstaff
Colleges: Northern Arizona Normal School, former name of Northern Arizona University (1915-1916)
MLB: 1922-1934
Clubs: Chicago Cubs (1922-1924); Pittsburgh Pirates (1925-1931); Cincinnati Reds (1932-1933); New York Giants (1934)
Bats: Left
Throws: Right
Games: 1,444; 1B (502); 2B (848); OF (19); 3B (14)
Average: .302
Home Runs: 105
RBIs: 712
Hits: 1,508
Runs: 912
Doubles: 292
Triples: 93
Stolen Bases: 132
Slugging Percentage: .461
On-Base Percentage: .392
Strikeouts: 526
Walks: 717
Fielding Percentage: .968; 1B (.988); 2B (.949)
World Series Appearances: 1925, 1927
World Series Champion: 1925
NAU Athletics Hall of Fame: 1986

Next is another infield reserve who dominated the 1950s in one particular, and painful, category. Hit by pitch.

He's Solly Hemus.

Like Jeremy Affeldt before him, Solomon Joseph Hemus was an Arizona native who grew up somewhere else. He was born in Phoenix in 1923, then moved to California, where he was a star player for St. Augustine High School in San Diego. Because of his service during World War II, he did not get his shot at the pros until 1946, when he signed with the St. Louis Cardinals at the age of 23. He started with the Pocatello Cardinals of the Pioneer League, where he put up a whopping .363 batting average. Hemus spent the next three seasons in the Texas League, playing for the Houston Buffaloes. In 1947, "The Little Pepper Pot," as fans called the 5'9, 165-pound infielder, hit .277 and helped the Buffs win the Dixie Series title. That earned him a spot in a March 22nd, 2012 *Houston Chronicle* article titled, "The Most Beloved Sports Figures in Houston History."

After batting .288 in 1948, Hemus made his major league debut on April 27th, 1949. He appeared as a pinch-hitter, grounding into a fielder's choice, as the Pirates clobbered the Cards 7-1.

With All-Stars Red Schoendienst and Marty Marion at second base and shortstop respectively, Hemus found it hard to get any regular playing time. He split time between the big club and the minors in 1949 and 1950.

1951, however, would be different. With Marion retiring to become the Cardinals manager, Hemus finally got his shot at being the everyday shortstop. He took advantage of his chance to shine, batting .281 with 68 runs scored, 18 doubles, nine triples and 32 RBIs. The next season was even more impressive. Hemus led the National League in not only runs scored with 105, but in hit by pitch, getting plunked 20 times. He also batted .268 with a .392 on-base percentage, 52 RBIs, 28 doubles and eight triples, while setting career highs in home runs with 15 and walks with 96. In 1953, he established career highs in RBIs with 61, doubles with 32, triples with eleven and runs scored with 110, which tied him for fifth most in the NL with future Hall of Famers Eddie Matthews of the Milwaukee Braves and Richie Ashburn of the Philadelphia Phillies.

In spite of all his success at the plate, Hemus was a bit error prone. He led the NL in miscues by a shortstop with 27 in 1953. That prompted the Cards to try rookie Alex Grammas at shortstop in 1954. His glove work proved a little better, and Hemus was relegated to the bench.

In 1956, the Cards traded Hemus to the Phillies for infielder Bobby Morgan. It was in Philadelphia he got to be a starter again . . . at least, half the time. Hemus platooned at second base with Granny Hamner his first two seasons in the City of Brotherly Love. In 1958, Hemus started the majority of games at second, batting .284 while scoring 53 runs in 105 games. That performance, however, wasn't enough to convince the Phillies to keep him. They dealt Hemus back to St. Louis, where he spent nearly all of the 1959 season on the bench . . . mainly because the Cardinals made him their player/manager. He only took advantage of the player part for 24 games, most of them as a pinch-hitter. The rest of the time he led his troops from the dugout. In 1960, Hemus officially declared an end to his playing days and concentrated solely on being St. Louis's skipper.

The success he enjoyed as a ballplayer never carried over to being a bench boss. In his three seasons at the helm of the Cardinals, he was 190-192 and never finished higher than third place in the National League. Hemus was replaced midway through the 1961 season by Johnny Keane, who went on to lead St. Louis to the 1964 World Championship. After coaching stints with the expansion New York Mets (1962-1963) and the Cleveland Indians (1964-1965), the Mets brought Hemus back to manage their AAA club, the Jacksonville Suns, in 1966. He only spent one year with them, going 68-79, before leaving pro baseball all together to start his second career, working in the oil business in Houston.

For St. Louis fans, whatever Hemus did during his playing career is probably overshadowed by what he did as their manager. In 1960, he made the controversial decision of benching Cardinal legend Stan Musial. Not just for one game, but for almost a month. Even though "Stan the Man" was batting around .200 and struggled defensively at first base, Hemus said in a September 12th, 1960 Sports Illustrated article, "I spent a lot of time, a lot of nights, worrying about this thing."

While the decision was hard for manager, player and fans, it seemed to pan out in the end. Hemus put the 39-year-old Musial back in the line-up in late June. The future Hall of Famer concluded the season batting .275 – twenty points higher than in 1959 – with 17 homers and 63 RBIs.

Career:
High School: St. Augustine (San Diego, CA)
MLB: 1949-1959
Clubs: St Louis Cardinals (1949-1956, 1959); Philadelphia Phillies (1956-1958)
Bats: Left
Throws: Right
Games: 961; SS (471); 2B (212); 3B (80)
Average: .273
Home Runs: 51
RBIs: 263
Hits: 736
Runs: 459
Doubles: 137
Triples: 41
Stolen Bases: 21
Slugging Percentage: .411
On-Base Percentage: .390
Strikeouts: 247
Walks: 456
Hit by Pitch: 62
Fielding Percentage: .966; SS (.962); 2B (.975)

League Leader Runs Scored: 1952 (105)
League Leader Hit by Pitch: 1952 (20), 1953 (12), 1958 (8)
St. Augustine High School Hall of Fame: 1995

The next reserve is another man who played high school, collegiate and pro ball in Arizona. He also may have been better at another sport besides baseball.

He's Mesa native Shea Hillenbrand.

One of the best athletes to ever come out of Mountain View High School, in his senior year he was named Arizona's player of the year . . . for soccer. Hillenbrand was also no slouch on the diamond, obviously, as that's where he made a name for himself professionally.

After graduating from Mountain View, he remained in his hometown, playing for Mesa Community College. He capped off a spectacular sophomore season in 1996 by being voted the Conference Player of the Year and selected to the NJCAA All-American First Team. That earned him attention from the Boston Red Sox, who selected him in the Tenth Round of the MLB Draft, 301st overall.

Hillenbrand tore through Single-A pitching, batting .315 for the Lowell Spinners in 1996 and a combined .293 with the Sarasota Red Sox and Michigan Battle Cats in 1997. Staying in Michigan in 1998, he wore out Midwest League pitching with a .349 batting average and 93 runs driven in, putting him second in the league in both categories.

With nothing more to prove in Single-A, the Red Sox promoted Hillenbrand to the AA Trenton Thunder in 1999. Unfortunately, an injury limited him to 69 games and a batting average of .259. He bounced back the next year, hitting .323 with 11 homers, 79 RBIs, 35 doubles and 77 runs for the Thunder. After a season like that, you might think his next stop would be AAA.

You'd be wrong. Hillenbrand's next stop was Boston.

After hitting .423 in spring training, he found himself in the starting line-up in the Sox 2001 season opener at Baltimore's Camden Yards. Hillenbrand got one of Boston's five hits that day as Pat Hentgen outdueled Pedro Martinez for a 2-1 Orioles win in eleven innings.

Hillenbrand had a decent rookie season, batting .263 with 12 home runs, 49 RBIs, 20 doubles and 52 runs scored. His sophomore season was much more than decent. Hillenbrand upped his average to .293 with 18 homers, 83 RBIs and career highs in doubles with 43 and runs scored with 94. He was also named the starting third baseman for the American League All-Star Team, where he went 0-2 in the infamous Mid-Summer Classic that ended in a 7-7 tie and heralded the start of the game's winner having home field advantage in the World Series.

That All-Star season, however, wasn't enough to keep him in Boston.

During the off-season, the Red Sox signed free agent Bill Mueller, who started the 2003 campaign in a platoon situation with Hillenbrand. That platoon turned into Mueller taking over the hot corner full-time after batting .418 for the month of May. This reportedly resulted in friction between Hillenbrand and Red Sox management.

It also resulted in his departure from Boston.

On May 29th, Hillenbrand was dealt to his home state team, the Arizona Diamondbacks, in exchange for pitcher Byung-Hyun Kim. Hillenbrand fared well in the desert. Splitting time between first and third base, he batted .267 with 17 home runs and 59 RBIs in 85 games.

In 2004, Arizona made him their starting first baseman. Again he put up good numbers, batting .310 with 15 homers, 80 RBIs, 68 runs scored and 36 doubles, making him the most productive player on a team that lost 111 games, just three years after winning it all.

Just like in Boston, good numbers did not keep him from being traded. On January 12th, 2005, Arizona sent Hillenbrand to Toronto for pitcher Adam Peterson, a once-promising reliever who only appeared in three games for AAA Tucson before being released. He never pitched in the pros again.

Hillenbrand, meanwhile, thrived north of the border. He batted .291 for the Jays with 18 home runs, 82 RBIs, 36 doubles and 91 runs scored. Hillenbrand was also named to his second All-Star team, and ended up the AL leader in the not-so pleasant category of hit-by-pitch, getting plunked 22 times. Everything appeared to be going well for him.

Then came the 2006 season. Hillenbrand claimed the Blue Jays were not accommodating when it came to granting him time off to finalize the adoption of his baby daughter. This led to a well-documented confrontation between him and Jays manager John Gibbons, the end result being Toronto designating Hillenbrand for assignment. He was later picked up by the San Francisco Giants, then spent 2007 with both Los Angeles teams. His production, however, suffered. He hit only .248 for the Giants and a combined .251 with four home runs and 31 RBIs for the Angels and Dodgers. Hillenbrand spent 2008 with the independent York Revolution, hung up his glove for four years, then tried to make a comeback with another independent team, the Bridgeport Bluefish, in 2012. He only lasted 29 games, hitting .194 before leaving the team.

According to an April, 2014 article in the *Portland Press Herald* titled, "Time for Contentment for Former Sox Malcontent," Hillenbrand has put his tumultuous baseball career behind him, accepted Christ into his life and works for a bat company.

Career:
High School: Mountain View (Mesa), Class of 1993
College: Mesa Community College (1995-1996)
MLB: 2001-2007
Clubs: Boston Red Sox (2001-2003); Arizona Diamondbacks (2003-2004); Toronto Blue Jays (2005-2006); San Francisco Giants (2006); Los Angeles Angels (2007); Los Angeles Dodgers (2007)
Bats: Right
Throws: Right

Games: 943; 3B (462); 1B (373); DH (125)
Average: .284
Home Runs: 108
RBIs: 490
Hits: 1,014
Runs: 463
Doubles: 202
Triples: 15
Stolen Bases: 16
Slugging Percentage: .440
On-Base Percentage: .321
Strikeouts: 464
Walks: 140
Hit by Pitch: 69
Fielding Percentage: .978; 1B (.991); 3B (.938)
League Leader Hit by Pitch: 2005 (22)
MLB All-Star: 2002, 2005
Mesa City Sports Hall of Fame: 2009

Now we come to the outfield reserves, and we start with a UofA product who might have put up huge numbers had it not been for injuries.

He's Hank Leiber.

Born in Phoenix in 1911, Leiber was a three-sport star not only in high school, but in college as well. He excelled in football, basketball and baseball at Phoenix High School, then did the same at the University of Arizona. At 6'1 and weighing over 200 pounds, he was named to the All-Southwestern Football Team as a fullback in 1930 and 1931. But of his three sports, baseball was his best, evidenced by the fact the New York Giants offered Leiber a contract 1932. He signed just a few credits shy of obtaining his degree. The Giants assigned him to the Class B Winston-Salem Twins and he tore up the Piedmont league, batting .362. The next season, the Giants brought him up to The Show.

Inserted into the starting line-up with future Hall of Famers Bill Terry and Mel Ott, Leiber went 2-5 with a run in his major league debut on April 16th, 1933. His run turned out to be the only one for New York as they and the Brooklyn Dodgers played to a 14-inning 1-1 tie.

Leiber played in only five more games after that, hitting .200, before going back to the minors. Splitting time between the Memphis Chickasaws and the Jersey City Skeeters, he hit .335. The Giants gave him another chance in the bigs in 1934. Leiber hit just .241 in 63 games. The next season, New York felt the ex-Wildcat showed enough promise that they made him their starting centerfielder.

That promise translated into one heck of a season. Leiber batted .331 with 22 home runs, 107 RBIs, 110 runs scored and 37 doubles, putting him in the top ten in the National League in all those categories. He also led the Giants in doubles and was second on the team in homers and RBIs behind Ott. Following that highly productive season, Leiber spent spring training of 1936 . . . not with the Giants. He held out for three weeks, trying to negotiate a better contract. According to a March 18th, 1936 *New York Post* article, the Phoenix native, who made around $7,500 the year before, was asking for $13,000. In the end, he settled for $11,000. The increase in pay, however, did not translate into an increase in his stats. Leiber batted .279 with just nine home runs, 67 RBIs and 44 runs scored.

While Leiber may not have lived up to expectations that year, his team did. The Giants went 92-62 to win the National League pennant. Next stop, the World Series versus the New York Yankees.

Game One saw a match-up of Hall of Famers, with Carl Hubbell outdueling the Yanks' Red Ruffing for a 6-1 Giants win. Leiber, however, watched the entire game from the bench. He got into the starting line-up for Game Two, going 0-4 as the Yankees stomped the Giants 18-4. He didn't see action again until Game Six, when he went 0-2 with a walk as the Pinstripes won in a 13-5 rout to capture the World Championship.

Leiber looked to rebound in 1937, but those plans were derailed by an 18-year-old pitcher for the Cleveland Indians named Bob Feller.

Not that he did this intentionally. During a spring training game in New Orleans, the "Heater from Van Meter" threw a curveball that got away from him. Leiber tried to duck, but the ball struck him in the head. This was during a time when batting helmets were unheard of in baseball. The result was a serious head injury that put Leiber in the hospital. Feller visited him there, and later called what happened an "unfortunate accident."

The head injury limited Leiber to 51 games in 1937, though he did bat .293. He also saw action in another World Series, again against the Yankees. Leiber's big October moment came in Game Five when he had a 2-run single in the Giants 8-1 victory. That would be their only win as the Yankees took the series in five games.

Still not 100% in 1938, Leiber hit .269 with 12 homers and 65 RBIs and was named to his first All-Star team. He got into the Mid-Summer Classic as a pinch-hitter for pitcher Johnny Vander Meer, who a month before threw back-to-back no-hitters for the Cincinnati Reds.

Because of injuries and declining stats, the Giants shipped off Leiber, along with two other All-Stars, shortstop Dick Bartell and catcher Gus Mancuso, to the Chicago Cubs for two more All-Stars, outfielder Frank Demaree and infielder Billy Jurges, and catcher Ken O'Dea. The trade worked wonders for Leiber. He played in 112 games in 1939, the first time he appeared in more than 100 games since 1936, hitting .310 with a career-high 24 home runs and 88 RBIs. The next season was just as successful as he hit .302 with 17 home runs, 86 RBIs, 68 runs scored and 24 doubles. Leiber was also named to his second NL All-Star Team, but did not appear in the game.

Just when his career looked back on track, Leiber suffered another beaning. This one occurred on June 24th, 1941. Playing against his former team, Giants pitcher Cliff Melton hit Leiber in the head so bad he said in an *Arizona Daily Star* article, "Babe Pinelli, the home plate umpire, later told me, 'I thought you were dead.'"

This second injury spelled the end of his career. Leiber was traded back to the Giants during the off-season, but only hit .218 in 58 games in 1942. At age 31, he called it quits.

Leiber enjoyed much success away from the diamond. He settled in Tucson, opened his own real estate agency and assisted in the development of a couple of country clubs. He was also a part-owner/manager of the Tucson Cowboys of the Arizona Texas League during the late 1940s.

Leiber passed away in 1993 at the age of 82. In his obituary, published in the *Arizona Daily Star* on November 9th of that year, Feller complimented the man he beaned decades earlier, saying, "He had a lot of power, very dangerous . . . The Hall of Fame should be considering him."

Leiber never got into Cooperstown, but he was inducted into the Arizona Sports Hall of Fame in 1963 and the University of Arizona Hall of Fame in 1977.

Career:
High School: Phoenix, Class of 1929
College: University of Arizona (1929-1931)
MLB: 1933-1942
Clubs: New York Giants (1933-1938, 1942); Chicago Cubs (1939-1941)
Bats: Right
Throws: Right
Games: 813; OF (698); 1B (28); P (1)
Average: .288
Home Runs: 101
RBIs: 518
Hits: 808
Runs: 410
Doubles: 137
Triples: 24
Slugging Percentage: .462
On-Base Percentage: .356
Stolen Bases: 5
Strikeouts: 319
Walks: 274
Fielding Percentage: .974; OF (.973); 1B (.982)
League Leader Hit-by-Pitch: 1935 (10)
MLB All-Star: 1938, 1940, 1941
World Series Appearances: 1936, 1937
Arizona Sports Hall of Fame: 1963
University of Arizona Hall of Fame: 1977

Next is a man who went from being a top performer on a cellar-dweller to a key member of a world championship team.

He is the versatile Mickey Hatcher.

Born in Cleveland, Hatcher and his family moved to Mesa, where he starred in baseball, basketball and football at Mesa High School. Not only was he an All-State player, he also made high school All-American teams in baseball and football. That success carried over to Mesa Community College. Hatcher not only achieved All-American status in both football and baseball, he helped the football team win the 1975 Junior College National Championship. One of his teammates at the time, Kelly Cordes, who played and coached varsity baseball at Prescott High School (1971-1973 and 1989-1995 respectively), said of Hatcher, "He was extremely competitive, but he was kind of a happy-go-lucky guy, too. I think that's probably why we called him 'Goofy.' Some of the guys on the team said the reason he came through in the clutch so much is because Hatcher didn't really understand when the pressure was on."

During his time at Mesa, Hatcher was drafted by the Houston Astros in 1974 and the New York Mets in 1975, but did not sign with either team. Instead, he continued his college football and baseball careers at the University of Oklahoma, where he served as a punter and wide receiver under Coach Barry Switzer. The Sooners were the co-champions of the Big Eight Conference, ended up fifth in the final AP National Poll and crushed Wyoming 41-7 in the 1976 Fiesta Bowl. When baseball season rolled around, Hatcher's performance earned him a spot on the All-American Second Team. It also got him drafted by the Los Angeles Dodgers in the Fifth Round, 124th overall. As an aside, also drafted in that round by the Yankees was an outfielder from Mississippi State. His name, Buck Showalter, the first ever manager in Arizona Diamondbacks history.

Hatcher's first stop in his pro career was in Clinton, Iowa, where he played for the Dodgers Single A affiliate. His teammates that year included a pair of future managers, Ron Roenicke (Brewers) and Mike Scioscia (Angels), Ron Kittle, who won the 1983 Rookie of the Year award, and Phoenix native Max Venable, who spent the majority of his 12-year major league career as a reserve outfielder for four different teams.

Hatcher had no trouble adjusting to the professional ranks. In 78 games for Clinton, he batted .309 with eleven homers, 53 RBIs, 47 runs scored and 14 steals. The next season he wore out AA and AAA pitching, hitting a combined .331 with 15 home runs, 101 RBIs, 85 runs scored, 23 doubles and 19 stolen bases for the San Antonio Dodgers and the Albuquerque Dukes. Staying in Albuquerque in 1979, Hatcher again put up big numbers, with a Pacific League best .371 batting average to go along with 93 RBIs and 88 runs scored. The Dodgers didn't bother waiting for September. They called up Hatcher in August. He made his major league debut on the 3rd of the month, coming in as a defensive replacement for third baseman Ron Cey. Hatcher had one plate appearance, walking with the bases loaded as Los Angeles crushed San Francisco 11-3. He finished the season batting .269 in 33 games.

Hatcher was back in AAA in 1980, but soon returned to L.A. However, with solid veterans like Steve Garvey, Ron Cey, Dusty Baker and Reggie Smith, and promising newcomers like Rudy Law and Pedro Guerrero, Hatcher found it difficult to get any playing time. He appeared in 42 games, mainly as a pinch-hitter or a late inning defensive replacement, and hit .226. Before the start of the 1981 season, Hatcher, along with minor leaguers Mathew Reeves and fellow Oklahoma product Kelly Snider, were traded to the Minnesota Twins for All-Star outfielder, and former ASU player, Ken Landreaux.

Hatcher batted .255 in 1981 and .249 in 1982. After that, he rediscovered his stroke, hitting over .300 in both 1983 and 1984 and posting a .282 average in 1985. Also that year, he collected hits in nine straight at-bats, tying the team record originally set by legendary Twins outfielder Tony Oliva.

While Hatcher did hit for a high average, the production he enjoyed in the minors did not translate to the big leagues. During that three-year span, he had more than 50 RBIs just once (69 in 1984) and scored more than 50 runs just once (61 in 1984). After hitting .278 in 1986, Hatcher was released by the Twins. In 1987, he returned to the team that had drafted him, the Los Angeles Dodgers. There he found his niche as a bench player, and flourished in that role. He batted .282 with 42 RBIs as a part-timer.

Then came 1988, the year Hatcher came through big for L.A. on more than one occasion.

During the regular season, he excelled as a pinch-hitter, posting a .316 average in 38 attempts. For the year, Hatcher hit .293 in 88 games. His part-time status changed to full-time in the 1988 National League Championship Series. Hatcher was the Dodgers starting first baseman in six of the seven games. His biggest moment came in Game Two, when he hit a two-run double in the second inning, then scored on Mike Marshall's RBI single as L.A. doubled-up the New York Mets 6-3. Hatcher batted .238 for the series with three RBIs and four runs scored as the Dodgers beat the Mets in seven games to win the NL Pennant. Next up was the Oakland A's, winners of 104 games that year. This marked Hatcher's first trip to the World Series, and he made the most of it.

Hatcher got the Dodgers on the board early in Game One with a two-run homer in the first inning off 21-game winner Dave Stewart. That game, however, would be remembered for another home run, the pinch-hit walk-off one off closer extraordinaire Dennis Eckersley by a hobbled Kirk Gibson, who served as Diamondbacks manager from 2010-2014.

Hatcher came up big again in Game Five with another first inning two-run homer off Storm Davis. The Dodgers took the game 5-2 and won their fifth – and at the time of publication, last – world championship since moving to Los Angeles in 1958. Hatcher batted .368 in the World Series with two home runs, five RBIs and five runs scored.

"When the game was on the line, there wasn't anyone at the plate you could depend on more than Mickey Hatcher," said Cordes. "I think he had that competitive spirit, although he was a fun-loving guy. Every time I thought of Hatcher, I just thought, gosh, he likes to go have fun. It seemed like he could go out and have fun and be serious and get the job done, all at the same time."

Hatcher spent two more seasons with the Dodgers, batting .295 in 1989, then .212 in 1990. He went to Albuquerque in 1991 to try to improve his stroke, but after hitting .160 in 17 games, he retired at age 36.

That didn't mean he was done with baseball. Hatcher spent two years (1993-1994) as the first base coach for the Texas Rangers before being hired as the manager of the rookie league Great Falls Dodgers. He led them to the Pioneer League Championship Series before taking over the Single A San Bernardino Stampede. Hatcher only lasted half the season, going 29-48 before being replaced. In 1999, he was hired by former Dodger teammate, and then Albuquerque manager, Mike Scioscia as the AAA team's hitting coach. When Scioscia became the Angels manager in 2000, he brought Hatcher with him as the hitting coach, a role he held until 2012. After his dismissal from the Angels, he was hired as a special assistant to Dodgers General Manager Ned Colletti.

Despite a lack of power in the majors, Hatcher proved a solid contact hitter who rarely struck out. His single-season high for whiffs was just 34 in 576 at-bats in 1984. He showed his versatility in the field by playing all three outfield positions, as well as first and third base. Hatcher also had a knack for keeping his teammates loose with his sense of humor. One example occurred during his second stint with the Dodgers. Hatcher created the "Bust Your Butt" award, which was presented to an L.A. player after every game. The award was not a plaque or a certificate. It was simply a photo of Hatcher mooning the cameraman.

Hatcher also owned a rather dubious record in high school sports, this one for basketball. Cordes said, "Hatcher was number one in committing the most fouls in his basketball career and also fouling out of the most games."

Career:
High School: Mesa, Class of 1974
Colleges: Mesa Community College (1974-1976); University of Oklahoma (1976-1977)
MLB: 1979-1990
Clubs: Los Angeles Dodgers (1979-1980, 1987-1990); Minnesota Twins (1981-1986)
Bats: Right
Throws: Right
Games: 1,130; OF (575), 1B (149), 3B (125), DH (145), P (1)
Average: .280
Home Runs: 38
RBIs: 375

Hits: 946
Runs: 348
Doubles: 172
Triples: 20
Slugging Percentage: .377
On-Base Percentage: .313
Stolen Bases: 11
Strikeouts: 246
Walks: 164
Fielding Percentage: .979; OF (.983); 1B (.989); 3B (.924)
League Leader Double Plays Turned as Leftfielder: 1986 (4)
World Series Championship: 1988
Mesa College Hall of Fame: 2008

Finally, we come to the back-up catcher. While not a bad defensive backstop, he was better known for his bat than his glove.

He's Terry Kennedy.

The son of sixteen-year major leaguer Bob Kennedy, Terry was born in Eulcid, Ohio in 1956, one year before his father retired as a player. Bob continued in baseball as both a minor and major league manager with the Salt Lake City Bees, the Chicago Cubs, the Arizona Instructional League Dodgers, the Albuquerque Dodgers and the Oakland A's. After living in Utah for a few years, the Kennedy family settled in Mesa, where Terry was a standout player at St. Mary's High School. After graduation, he headed east to play for Florida State. All he did there was re-write the Seminole record book. During his sophomore season, he set single-season records in home runs and RBIs with 21 and 64. He also had an .810 slugging percentage, still a school single-season record. In his three years at Florida State, Kennedy socked 32 home runs and drove in 122 runs. He also earned spots on *The Sporting News* All-American First Team in 1976 and 1977, the year the Seminoles won the Metro Conference Championship.

The St. Louis Cardinals selected Kennedy in the First Round of the 1977 MLB Draft, sixth overall. He was in pretty good company in that draft, as other First Round selections included long-time White Sox designated hitter Harold Baines (#1), Hall of Famer Paul Molitar (#3) and future post-season hero Dave Henderson (#26).

Kennedy was assigned to the rookie league Johnson City Cardinals, playing just 12 games with them. The reason? He hit .590 with three homers, 15 RBIs and 14 runs scored in that very short span. Then, just like that, Kennedy was in Single A, finishing out the '77 season with the St. Petersburg Cardinals. He came back down to earth in the Florida State League, batting .247 with 22 RBIs. The next year, he split his time in the minors with the AA Arkansas Travelers and the AAA Springfield Redbirds, batting a combined .309 with 20 homers, 100 RBIs, 90 runs scored and 27 doubles. Kennedy was a September call-up, debuting for the

Cards on the 4th of that month. He pinch-hit for Ted Simmons in the eighth inning and promptly grounded out. St. Louis lost that game to the Phillies 10-2. Kennedy played in nine more games in 1978, hitting just .172.

After another successful stint in Springfield, where he hit .293 with 13 homers and 64 RBIs, he was called up again by the Cardinals. But with Simmons locked in as the starting catcher, Kennedy was relegated to a utility role. In December, 1980, Kennedy was part of a massive eleven-player trade between the Cardinals and Padres. It was in San Diego where the former number one draft pick finally had the chance to showcase his talents.

Even though the Padres struggled, Kennedy did not. In 101 games during the strike-shortened 1981 season, he hit .301 with two homers, 41 RBIs, 24 doubles and 32 runs scored. He was also San Diego's lone representative at the 1981 All-Star Game, where he appeared as a pinch-hitter.

The next two seasons were some of the most productive of Kennedy's big league career. In 1982, he hit .295 with 97 RBIs and posted career highs in home runs with 21, doubles with 42 and runs scored with 75. He then achieved a career high in RBIs in 1983 with 98 while batting .284 with 17 home runs. Kennedy was named to his second All-Star team and received a Silver Slugger award as the best hitting catcher in the National League.

1984, however, saw Kennedy's stats take a nosedive. He batted just .240 with 14 homers and 57 RBIs. Despite his slump, the Padres won the NL West, then went on to defeat the Chicago Cubs in five games in the NLCS. Kennedy's struggles with the stick continued in the post-season as he batted .222 with just one RBI in the playoffs.

He made up for that lack of production when San Diego got to the World Series against heavily favored Detroit. In Game One, Kennedy went 2-4, his big hit a two-run double off Tigers' ace Jack Morris in the first inning, giving the Padres an early 2-1 lead. Detroit, however, came back to win the game 3-2. In Game Four, Kennedy got to Morris again, this time with a solo home run to pull the Padres within one of the Tigers in the second inning. Detroit, however, won the game 4-2 and won the series in five games.

Kennedy rebounded in 1985, hitting .261 with ten homers, 74 RBIs, 54 runs scored and 27 doubles. He was also named the starting catcher of the National League All-Star team and came through with an RBI single against, of all pitchers, Jack Morris. The NL won the Mid-Summer Classic that year 6-1. Kennedy caught the first four innings before being replaced by another Arizona product, Moon Valley High School graduate Ozzie Virgil, who played for the Phillies that year. Virgil also did the Grand Canyon State proud that night, hitting a two-run single off Bert Blyleven.

After a decent 1986 season (.264, 12 HR, 57 RBIs, 46 R, 22 2B), Kennedy was dealt to Baltimore along with pitcher Mark Williamson for pitcher Storm Davis. The St. Mary's grad did well his first season with the Orioles, batting .250 with 18 home runs, 62 RBIs and 51 runs scored. He also made his fourth All-Star team, again as the starting catcher, and wound up as Jack Morris's battery mate for a couple of innings.

Kennedy saw his playing time diminish in 1988 when Baltimore brought in slugging catcher Mickey Tettleton. The two split time behind the dish, with Kennedy batting just .226 in 85 games. At the end of the season, he was traded to San Francisco for catcher, and future Diamondbacks manager, Bob Melvin. Even though his offense was in decline – he hit just .239 in 1989 – Kennedy was still a solid defensive backstop and helped the Giants win the NL West. They beat the Cubs in five games, with Kennedy hitting under the Mendoza line at .188 with no RBIs. He also hit just .167 in the infamous "Earthquake Series," driving in two runs as Oakland swept San Francisco.

Kennedy got his average back up to .277 in 1990, but it dropped to .234 the next season. Following the 1991 campaign, Kennedy retired. As of 2014, he is tied for seventh on the Padres all-time list in doubles, eighth in RBIs and at-bats, and ninth in hits and games played.

Shortly after his retirement, Kennedy returned to baseball, spending much of the 1990s and 2000s as a minor league manager. His stops included the St. Petersburg Cardinals (1993), the Vermont Expos (1994), the Iowa Cubs (1998-1999), the Las Vegas 51s (2004), the San Antonio Missions (2009) and the Portland Beavers (2010). He even skippered the San Diego Surf Dawgs of the independent Golden Baseball League in 2005 and 2006. Kennedy also put in managerial time in his adopted home state. In 1997, he helmed the Arizona Rookie League Cubs, then wrapped up his managing career with the Tucson Padres in 2011 and 2012.

Career:
High School: St. Mary's (Phoenix) Class of 1974
College: Florida State University (1975-1977)
MLB: 1978-1991
Clubs: St. Louis Cardinals (1978-1980); San Diego Padres (1981-1986); Baltimore Orioles (1987-1988); San Francisco Giants (1989-1991)
Bats: Left
Throws: Right
Games: 1,491; C (1,378); OF (28); 1B (25)
Average: .264
Home Runs: 113
RBIs: 628
Hits: 1,313
Runs: 474
Doubles: 244
Triples: 12
Slugging Percentage: .386
On-Base Percentage: .314

Stolen Bases: 6
Strikeouts: 855
Walks: 365
Fielding Percentage: .986
Runners Thrown out Stealing: 478
MLB All-Star: 1981, 1983, 1985, 1987
League Leader Runners Caught Stealing: 1981 (48), 1987 (49)
League Leader Assists by Catcher: 1987 (58)
League Leader Double Plays Turned as Catcher: 1981 (12), 1982 (11), 1985 (12)
World Series Appearances: 1984, 1989
Florida State University Hall of Fame: 1982

MANAGER

Now that the players are assembled, we need someone to lead them. Candidates for that job are few and far between when restricting the search to Arizona. The only man born in the state who had any major league managerial experience was mentioned a few pages back, Solly Hemus. But his career record as a skipper was 190-192. So for this section we turn our search to the college ranks, more specifically, to Tempe. The manager for Arizona's All-Time Baseball Team is someone who is a legendary figure in ASU baseball and one of the winningest coaches in the NCAA.

He's Jim Brock.

The Phoenix-born head coach was no stranger to managing big league caliber talent. During his tenure at Arizona State, more than sixty of his charges went on to play in the majors. They include Barry Bonds, Bump Wills, Floyd Bannister, Hubie Brooks, Marty Barrett, Alvin Davis, Fernando Vina and one of starters for the All-Time Arizona Team, Bob Horner.

But had things been different, Brock may not have even been considered for this spot. That's because he was only expected to serve one season as ASU's head coach.

Before assuming the mantle of Sun Devil skipper, Brock was a standout pitcher for North High School in Phoenix. After spending two years at Phoenix College, he transferred to ASU, where he earned his bachelor's degree in physical education in 1958. While most people begin coaching after their college days are over, Brock became a bench boss while still in college. He took over the reins of the Kerr's Sporting Goods American Legion team from his father, Bill, in 1956. It wasn't long before he earned a reputation as not only a taskmaster, but someone who had a great mind for the game despite his young age.

His wife Pat explained, "He wanted to be a coach from the time he was a very young boy. He didn't aspire to play baseball in the big leagues or anything like that."

After spending a year working in California, the Brocks returned to Arizona, where Jim again led the Kerr's Legion team. Not only did they win the state championship in 1961, they also won the national championship.

The next year, Brock was hired as the head coach at Mesa High School. Two years later, he made the jump to the collegiate ranks when he became the first head coach for Mesa College. All this before he was even 30.

On his Hall of Fame plaque for Mesa, his wife said that Brock, "Couldn't live with losing." That same plaque also described him as "A holy terror when his team lost." It's probably the reason why the HoKams did not lose much during Brock's tenure. In his six seasons at Mesa, they won 75% of their games. They also won three conference championships and the ultimate prize, the junior college national championship in 1970 and 1971.

At the height of his success, Brock walked away from the HoKams, deciding to take a sabbatical in order to finish his doctorate in education administration from ASU. He served as an intern for Athletic Director Fred Miller and was considering a career as a high school principal when the UofA head coach's job became available. Despite his success at Mesa, Brock didn't get hired. Shortly after he returned from Tucson, he learned that another head coaching job had opened up.

It was the one at ASU.

He got that job, but many in the ASU universe felt there was no way Brock could succeed. He had no prior NCAA coaching experience. Plus he was replacing a man, Bobby Winkles, who built the Sun Devil baseball program from scratch and turned it into a three-time national champion. Those weren't big shoes to fill. Those were enormous shoes.

To many people's surprise, Brock filled them. ASU went 64-6 in 1972 and were the national runner-up, losing in the championship game to USC 1-0.

Five years later, in 1977, he led a team that included future major leaguers Bob Horner, Hubie Brooks and Chris Bando back to the College World Series, and this time ASU won it. In 1981, the Sun Devils captured another CWS title. This made Brock the only coach in history to win national championships in the American Legion, junior college and NCAA ranks.

So what were some of the reasons for Brock's success? According to Pat, "He had high standards. He expected a lot from the kids as far as their personal appearance, their demeanor on the field, and of course, their performance during games and also during practice. He never went to practice without a detailed, many-page schedule. He was driven. He wanted to win. Even when we won the National Championship one year, we went on vacation right away to Hawaii, and that was a bad mistake, because all he could think about was who he was losing and who we needed for next year."

The success continued for ASU under Brock's leadership. He led his team to eleven conference championships and 13 appearances in the College World Series, where along with the national titles, they were also national runners-up in 1972, 1973, 1978 and 1988.

Going into his 23rd season as ASU's skipper, Brock went up against an opponent tougher than any he ever faced on the field.

Cancer.

Despite having a most of his liver removed, the cancer remained. Still, Brock coached the Sun Devils to the 1994 CWS. In their first game, they shut out Miami 4-0. Three days later, ASU met the Hurricanes again.

Coach Brock, however, wasn't there for the game.

His condition took a turn for the worse, forcing him to return to a Phoenix area hospital. Five days later, he passed away at the age of 57.

While he had a reputation as a fiery and demanding head coach who routinely butted heads with umpires, other coaches and administrators, his personality never seemed to have a negative impact on his teams. Pat pointed out, "Many of them say Coach Brock gave me the discipline I needed and helped me be the person I am today. They played afterwards for other coaches in minor league ball or major league baseball, and they realized you have to have that discipline and you have to have high standards."

Brock's high standards and discipline paid off as he won 1,100 games as the Sun Devils head coach. He was also a four-time NCAA National Coach of the Year, a five-time Pac-10 Coach of the Year, and coached all three of ASU's Golden Spikes Award winners, Horner (1978), Oddibe McDowell (1984) and Mike Kelly (1991). In 2007, Brock was inducted into the College Baseball Hall of Fame.

Brock's methods of discipline could be out of the ordinary, as Pat explained, "Our JV team was down in Yuma playing a game, and one of our players who was a pitcher was down in the bullpen and some friends came along to visit him and one offered him a sip of beer from his beer can. An ASU fan saw that and called my husband on Monday morning. Jim made that young man run a hundred miles before he could put his uniform on again, and that young man is a big fan of my husband today."

Career:
High School: North (Phoenix): Class of 1954
College: Mesa College (1954-1956); ASU (1956-1958)
Years Active as Manager: 1962-1994
Schools: Mesa High School (1962-1964); Mesa College (1966-1971); ASU (1972-1994)
Record: Mesa College (163-80-2); ASU (1,100-440)

Conference Titles: Mesa College (1969, 1970, 1971); ASU (1972, 1973, 1975, 1976, 1977, 1978, 1981, 1982, 1984, 1988, 1993)
World Series Appearances: Mesa College (1969, 1970, 1971); ASU (1972, 1973, 1975, 1976, 1977, 1978, 1981, 1983, 1984, 1987, 1988, 1993, 1994)
National Championships: Mesa College (1970, 1971); ASU (1977, 1981)
Pac-10 Coach of the Year: 1981, 1982, 1984, 1988, 1993
Junior College National Coach of the Year: 1970, 1971
NCAA National Coach of the Year: 1977, 1981, 1984, 1988
Mesa College Hall of Fame: 2006
ASU Hall of Fame: 1994
College Baseball Hall of Fame: 2007

STARTING LINEUP

1 – Billy Hatcher, CF (R)
2 – Ian Kinsler, 2B (R)
3 – Bob Horner, 3B (R)
4 – Paul Konerko, 1B (R)
5 – Tim Salmon, RF (R)
6 – Andre Ethier, LF (L)
7 – J.J. Hardy, SS (R)
8 – Tom Pagnozzi, C (R)

STARTING ROTATION

#1 – Jim Palmer (R)
#2 – Curt Schilling (R)
#3 – John Denny (R)
#4 – Gary Gentry (R)
#5 – Gil Heredia (R)

BULLPEN

Bob Milacki – Long and Middle Relief/Emergency Starter (R)
Alex Kellner – Long and Middle Relief/Emergency Starter (L)
Lerrin LaGrow – Middle Relief/Set-up (R)
Jeremy Affeldt – Set-up (L)
Bobby Howry – Set-up (R)
Mike MacDougal – Closer (R)

BENCH

George Grantham – 1B/2B/3B/OF (L)
Solly Hemus – SS/2B/3B (L)
Shea Hillenbrand – 3B/1B (R)
Hank Leiber – OF/1B (R)
Mickey Hatcher – OF/3B/1B (R)
Terry Kennedy – C/OF/1B (L)

So there you have it. Arizona's All-Time Baseball Team. No doubt you are thinking, "How would a team like this do in actual games?" Why wonder when we can actually see? Using my old Strat-O-Matic game, I have pitted Arizona's best players against the 2001 New York Yankees, who faced the Arizona Diamondbacks in that year's World Series, in a best-of-seven series.

Time for baseball history to come alive.

ARIZONA'S ALL-TIME BASEBALL TEAM VS. 2001 NEW YORK YANKEES

Game One: Chase Field

The opener of this series saw two of the greatest pitchers of their generations face-off. On the bump for Arizona was Jim Palmer, and opposing him was Roger Clemens. The two hurlers brought a combined ten Cy Young Awards, 17 All Star appearances, 6,884 strikeouts and fourteen 20-win seasons to the ballpark, setting the stage for one of the greatest pitchers duels ever.

The duel, however, started with the Yankees giving Palmer and the rest of the Arizona nine a heck of a scare.

Derek Jeter got a one-out single in the top of the first. After David Justice struck out, Bernie Williams laced the ball to right-center field for a double. Jeter raced around third, heading for home. But Tim Salmon's throw from right was on target. Tom Pagnozzi caught the ball on one bounce and applied the tag to Jeter, ending the inning.

Clemens didn't have to deal with much of a scare in his first inning of work. While he did walk Bob Horner, The Rocket struck out Billy Hatcher, Ian Kinsler and Paul Konerko.

The 0-0 score didn't last long. After Tino Martinez and Jorge Posada were retired in the top of the second, Alfonso Soriano socked one into the left field stands to put New York on top 1-0.

Palmer struck out Clemens to start the third inning, then walked Chuck Knoblauch, with Jeter up next. But the Yankee shortstop hit a grounder to J.J. Hardy, who turned a 6-4-3 double play. Threat avoided.

Palmer led off the bottom of the third for Arizona. While Clemens already had punchouts of sluggers like Konerko and Salmon in the first two innings, he wound up walking his opposite number.

That walk came back to bite Clemens. After getting Hatcher to pop out, Clemens served up a fastball that Kinsler blasted out of the park to put Arizona on top 2-1.

The Rocket gave up another leadoff walk in the fourth, this one to Hardy. After fanning Pagnozzi, Palmer bunted back to the mound. Clemens picked up the ball, spun around and threw to second. But the throw was off target and both Hardy and Palmer were safe. Next up was Hatcher, who drove the ball to left-center field to score Hardy and make it 3-1 Arizona.

After Kinsler struck out, Clemens walked Horner for the second time, loading the bases and giving a chance for Konerko to break the game open. The slugging first baseman, instead, went down swinging to end the inning.

Palmer, meanwhile, settled down, getting the Yankees in order in the fourth and fifth innings. In the bottom of the fifth, Arizona got to Clemens again as Salmon led off with a homer to left-center field, making the score 4-1.

Clemens's night ended in the top of the sixth as Enrique Wilson pinch hit for him and delivered a leadoff double. The Yankees now had a runner in scoring position and no outs, with the top of the order coming up.

Knoblauch grounded to third, Jeter flew out to left and Justice hit a liner into Hardy's glove, leaving Wilson stranded at second.

New York threatened again in the seventh. After Williams grounded out, Martinez and Posada hit back-to-back singles, putting runners at the corners with one out. Soriano hit a fly ball to center that Hatcher caught, but it was too shallow for the not-so speedy Martinez to score from third. It was up to Scott Brosius to try and cut into the Arizona lead, but he grounded to Horner, who threw out Posada at second to end the inning.

Knowing that a three-run lead was not safe against an offense as potent as New York's, Arizona manager Jim Brock opted to give Hatcher the green light to steal after a leadoff walk in the eighth. His speed, however, was no match for Posada's arm as the Yankee backstop gunned him down at second. That was followed by Kinsler striking out. Just when it appeared reliever Jay Witasick would get out of the inning unscathed, Horner struck for Arizona's third home run of the night to increase their lead 5-1.

The Yankees, though, had the heart of their order due up in the top of the ninth.

Palmer returned to the hill, looking to finish out the game. First up was Justice, who flew out to right. Williams then grounded out to second. That made Tino Martinez the last hope for the Yanks. With his power, and with Posada and Soriano behind him in the order, New York was by no means out of it.

Martinez hit a bouncer down the third baseline. Solly Hemus, who came in as a defensive replacement for Horner, snagged it and threw to first for the final out, giving Arizona's All-Time Baseball Team the 5-1 victory to begin this best-of-seven series.

2001 NY Yankees

	AB	R	H	2B	3B	HR	RBI	K	BB
Chuck Knoblauch - LF	3	0	0	0	0	0	0	0	1
Derek Jeter - SS	4	0	1	0	0	0	0	0	0
David Justice – RF	4	0	0	0	0	0	0	1	0
Bernie Williams – CF	4	0	1	1	0	0	0	0	0
Tino Martinez – 1B	4	0	1	0	0	0	0	1	0
Jorge Posada – C	3	0	1	0	0	0	0	0	0
Alfonso Soriano – 2B	3	1	1	0	0	1	1	0	0
Scott Brosius – 3B	3	0	0	0	0	0	0	0	0
Roger Clemens – P	1	0	0	0	0	0	0	1	0
Enrique Wilson – PH (6th)	1	0	1	1	0	0	0	0	0
Ramiro Mendoza – P (6th)	0	0	0	0	0	0	0	0	0
Shane Spencer – PH (8th)	1	0	0	0	0	0	0	0	0
Jay Witasick – P (8th)	0	0	0	0	0	0	0	0	0
Mike Stanton – P (8th)	0	0	0	0	0	0	0	0	0

LOB: 3

AZ All-Time Team

	AB	R	H	2B	3B	HR	RBI	K	BB
Billy Hatcher – CF	4	0	1	1	0	0	1	1	1
Ian Kinsler – 2B	5	1	2	0	0	1	2	3	0
Bob Horner – 3B	3	1	2	0	0	1	1	1	2
Solly Hemus – 3B (9th)	0	0	0	0	0	0	0	0	0
Paul Konerko – 1B	4	0	0	0	0	0	0	3	1
Tim Salmon – RF	5	1	3	1	0	1	1	1	0
Andre Ethier – LF	4	0	1	0	0	0	0	1	1
Mickey Hatcher – LF (9th)	0	0	0	0	0	0	0	0	0
J.J. Hardy – SS	3	1	0	0	0	0	0	0	1
Tom Pagnozzi – C	4	0	2	0	0	0	0	1	0
Jim Palmer – P	3	1	0	0	0	0	0	2	1

CS: B. Hatcher
LOB: 11

PITCHING:

2001 NY Yankees	IP	R	ER	H	HR	K	BB
Roger Clemens (L)	5	4	4	6	2	10	5
Ramiro Mendoza	2	0	0	3	0	2	0
Jay Witasick	2/3	1	1	1	1	1	2
Mike Stanton	1/3	0	0	1	0	0	0

AZ All-Time Team	IP	R	ER	H	HR	K	BB
Jim Palmer (W)	9	1	1	5	0	3	1

	1	2	3	4	5	6	7	8	9	R	H	E
'01 NY Yankees	0	1	0	0	0	0	0	0	0	1	5	0
AZ All-Time Team	0	0	2	1	1	0	0	1	X	5	11	0

Game Two: Chase Field

After managing only five hits in Game One, the Yankees were determined to get to Arizona starter Curt Schilling early. And they did.

At least, one New York batter did.

Chuck Knoblauch led off the game with a double, but second base is where he'd stay as the next three batters – Derek Jeter, David Justice and Bernie Williams – all flied out.

Arizona's leadoff batter also got on in the first inning, as Knoblauch had a fly ball pop out of his glove, allowing Billy Hatcher to make it to second base. Like Knoblauch in the top of the inning, Hatcher never reached third. Mike Mussina fanned both Ian Kinsler and Bob Horner before getting Paul Konerko to ground out.

Still scoreless in the third, Scott Brosius led off with a single. Mussina attempted to bunt him over to second, but instead popped out to Schilling. Knoblauch and Jeter both grounded out to end the inning.

Errors in the outfield bit the Yanks again in the bottom of the third. Tom Pagnozzi's leadoff single skipped off Bernie Williams's glove, allowing the Arizona catcher to reach second. Schilling laid down a bunt, allowing his battery mate to advance to third.

Up came Hatcher, with a chance to break the scoreless tie. Instead, he grounded to Jeter at short, and Pagnozzi was forced to stay at third. Next up was Kinsler, who had a two-run blast in Game One. The Canyon del Oro grad came through again, smacking a single to left-center field to drive in Pagnozzi and put Arizona up 1-0.

Schilling struck out the side in the top of the fourth, with the only blemish a Williams single. In the bottom of the inning, Konerko, who went 0-4 with three strikeouts in Game One, made up for it by knocking the ball into the Chase Field pool to give Arizona a 2-0 lead. But the offense wasn't done there. After Tim Salmon's flyout to center, Andre Ethier doubled, then came home on a J.J. Hardy single. Pagnozzi followed with another single, then advanced to second on Schilling's bunt. With runners on second and third, Arizona had a chance to blow the game open.

But Mussina overcame his struggles and fanned Hatcher to end the inning, though with Arizona now on top 3-0.

The Yankees began the fifth inning with their third leadoff hit of the game, as Alfonso Soriano singled to left. Desperate to get a runner in scoring position, Soriano attempted to steal second, but was gunned down by Pagnozzi on a strike 'im out, throw 'im out double play. Schilling fanned Mussina for the third out, and set down the side in order in the sixth.

Arizona started off the home half of the sixth inning with a single by Salmon, who was thrown out at second when Ethier hit into a fielder's choice. After Hardy popped out to Jeter, Pagnozzi singled to right, and Ethier made it third. Next up was Schilling, who attempted to lay down his third bunt of the game. When the count reached two strikes, Manager Jim Brock let him swing away.

Schilling did not disappoint. The career .151 hitter stroked the ball into left-center field, plating Ethier and upping Arizona's lead over New York 4-0.

The Yanks finally touched up Schilling in the seventh, as Jorge Posada jacked a solo shot over the left-centerfield fence to make it a 4-1 game.

The New York bullpen took over for Mussina and pitched lights out, with Jay Witasick retiring the side in order in the seventh and Ramiro Mendoza doing the same in the eighth.

In the top of the ninth, Brock elected to leave Schilling in to finish the game, though he did have Mike MacDougal up in the bullpen just in case. Jeter led off the inning with a single, and given the Yankees history of late inning comebacks, no doubt the fans at Chase Field were nervous.

Brock, though, was not, as he stuck with Schilling.

The next batter was Justice, who flew out to right for out number one. Next came Williams, who grounded to short. Hardy's only play was to second to get the force on Jeter.

Down to their last out, up came Tino Martinez, one of New York's most productive hitters in 2001 with a .280 average, 34 home runs and 113 RBIs. Behind him in the order were Posada and Soriano. The Yankees still had a shot at a comeback.

But Schilling would have none of that. He got Martinez swinging for his tenth strikeout of the night and Arizona's All-Time Team got the 4-1 win to take a two games to none lead over the Yankees.

2001 NY Yankees	AB	R	H	2B	3B	HR	RBI	K	BB
Chuck Knoblauch – LF	4	0	1	1	0	0	0	0	0
Ramiro Mendoza – P (8th)	0	0	0	0	0	0	0	0	0
Derek Jeter – SS	4	0	1	0	0	0	0	0	0
David Justice – RF	4	0	0	0	0	0	0	1	0
Bernie Williams – CF	4	0	1	0	0	0	0	1	0
Tino Martinez – 1B	4	0	0	0	0	0	0	3	0
Jorge Posada – C	3	1	1	0	0	1	1	1	0
Alfonso Soriano – 2B	3	0	1	0	0	0	0	2	0
Scott Brosius – 3B	3	0	1	0	0	0	0	1	0
Mike Mussina – P	2	0	0	0	0	0	0	1	0
Jay Witasick – P (7th)	0	0	0	0	0	0	0	0	0
Paul O'Neill – PH/LF (8th)	0	0	0	0	0	0	0	0	1

ERR: Knoblauch, Williams
CS: Soriano, O'Neill
LOB: 4

AZ All-Time Team	AB	R	H	2B	3B	HR	RBI	K	BB
Billy Hatcher – CF	4	0	0	0	0	0	0	2	0
Ian Kinsler – 2B	4	0	1	0	0	0	1	2	0
Bob Horner – 3B	4	0	0	0	0	0	0	2	0
Shea Hillenbrand – 3B (9th)	0	0	0	0	0	0	0	0	0
Paul Konerko – 1B	4	1	1	0	0	1	1	0	0
Tim Salmon – RF	4	0	1	0	0	0	0	0	0
Andre Ethier – LF	4	2	1	1	0	0	0	1	0
J.J. Hardy – SS	4	0	1	0	0	0	1	0	0
Tom Pagnozzi – C	3	1	3	0	0	0	0	0	0
Curt Schilling – P	1	0	1	0	0	0	1	0	0

SAC: Schilling (2)
LOB: 5

PITCHING:

2001 NY Yankees	IP	R	ER	H	HR	K	BB
Mike Mussina (L)	6	4	4	9	1	5	0
Jay Witasick	1	0	0	0	0	2	0
Ramiro Mendoza	1	0	0	0	0	0	0

AZ All-Time Team	IP	R	ER	H	HR	K	BB
Curt Schilling (W)	9	1	1	6	1	10	1

	1	2	3	4	5	6	7	8	9	R	H	E
'01 NY Yankees	0	0	0	0	0	0	1	0	0	1	6	2
AZ All-Time Team	0	0	1	2	0	1	0	0	X	4	9	0

Game Three: Yankee Stadium

John Denny took the mound for Arizona as the series moved east, but the 1983 Cy Young winner got off to a shaky start. In the bottom of the first, he walked leadoff hitter Chuck Knoblauch, who promptly stole second. Derek Jeter followed with a grounder to second, allowing Knoblauch to advance to third. Next came Paul O'Neill, who got the start in right for this game. The move paid immediate dividends as he smacked a fly ball to right that brought home Knoblauch to put New York up 1-0.

Yankee starter Andy Pettitte had no trouble with the Arizona lineup. He retired the first seven batters he saw and faced one over the minimum through the first four innings, striking out four.

In the bottom of the fourth, New York got another leadoff hitter on as J.J. Hardy mishandled a grounder from O'Neill, allowing the Yankee right fielder to make it to second. Next up was Bernie Williams, who slapped the ball to right for a base hit to drive in O'Neill for a 2-0 lead. Denny got Tino Martinez to ground into a double play, then ended the inning by striking out Jorge Posada.

Arizona had an opportunity to cut into the Yankee lead in the fifth. After a Bob Horner groundout, Tim Salmon drew a walk. Hardy came up and stroked a single to the opposite field. Salmon rounded second and charged to third. O'Neill threw a bullet to second baseman Alfonso Soriano, who spun and threw to third. Scott Brosius snagged the ball and put the tag on Salmon, erasing him from the base paths. Mickey Hatcher came up next and singled to left, putting runners on first and second with two down and Tom Pagnozzi up. A combined 5-7 in the first two games, Arizona was hoping for a big hit from their catcher.

Instead, Pettitte got Pagnozzi swinging on a curveball for strike three, preserving the Yanks 2-0 lead.

In the bottom of the fifth, Denny again had trouble keeping the leadoff man off base as he walked designated hitter Shane Spencer. Soriano followed with a single, giving New York two on with nobody out. Next came Brosius, with a chance to widen the lead.

Instead, the ninth place hitter grounded into a 6-4-3 double play. Still, Spencer made it to third, with Knoblauch at bat. A fastball that just hit the inside corner of the plate froze him for strike three as Denny worked himself out of the jam.

Pettitte fanned Billy Hatcher to start the top of the sixth. Next came Ian Kinsler, who belted a Pettitte curveball into the left-centerfield stands for his second homer of the series. Hank Leiber, who was in the lineup as Arizona's DH, singled, then went to third on Paul Konerko's double. Pettitte tried to regain control of the game as he faced Bob Horner, who was 0-2 at that point. The Apollo High grad hit a fly ball to deep left, driving in Leiber to tie the game 2-2. Tim Salmon tried to keep the offense going, but flew out to left to end the inning.

The tie, however, did not last long.

In the bottom of the sixth, O'Neill put one into the right field porch with one out to give the Yankees the lead again, 3-2. Denny avoided further damage by fanning Bernie Williams and getting Tino Martinez to fly out to center.

The bullpen took over for Pettitte in the top of the seventh. Even though Randy Choate gave up a leadoff single to Hardy, he got Mickey Hatcher and Pagnozzi to ground into fielder's choices. Billy Hatcher, however, singled to keep the inning alive. Then Kinsler walked to load the bases with two outs. Up came Leiber, 1-3 on the day. Choate ran the count to 1-2 on the DH and was on the verge of getting out of the inning. Leiber, however, smoked the ball down the left field line, scoring Pagnozzi and Hatcher and giving Arizona a 4-3 lead. Konerko batted next and singled in Kinsler to make it 5-3. That brought an end to Choate's night. He was replaced by Sterling Hitchcock, who just needed to get Horner out to end the inning.

The former ASU standout, however, blasted a three-run home run into the left field stands. Salmon made it back-to-back jacks to knock Hitchcock out of the game. Mike Stanton came out of the bullpen to try and hold back the flood, but gave up a double to Hardy. He managed to strike out Mickey Hatcher for out number three, but the Yankees now found themselves in a 9-3 hole.

For the first time in the series, Manager Jim Brock used his bullpen. Bob Milacki threw two shutout innings. Jeremy Affeldt came on to pitch the ninth. Down six runs, the Yanks still showed signs of life as Martinez led off with a single. He was erased when Posada grounded into a 4-6-3 double play. It all came down to DH David Justice to keep New York alive, but Affeldt set him down on strikes to end the game 9-3 in Arizona's favor and give them a commanding 3-0 lead in the series.

AZ All-Time Team	AB	R	H	2B	3B	HR	RBI	K	BB
Billy Hatcher – CF	5	1	1	0	0	0	0	1	0
Ian Kinsler – 2B	4	1	2	1	0	1	1	1	1
Hank Leiber – DH	5	2	3	0	0	0	2	1	1
Paul Konerko – 1B	4	1	2	1	0	0	1	0	0
Terry Kennedy – PH/1B (9th)	1	0	0	0	0	0	0	0	0
Bob Horner – 3B	3	1	1	0	0	1	4	0	0
Solly Hemus – 3B (7th)	1	0	0	0	0	0	0	1	0
Tim Salmon – RF	3	1	1	0	0	1	1	0	1
George Grantham – RF (9th)	1	0	1	0	0	0	0	0	0
J.J. Hardy – SS	5	0	4	1	0	0	0	2	0
Mickey Hatcher – LF	5	0	2	0	0	0	0	2	0
Tom Pagnozzi – C	4	1	0	0	0	0	0	2	0

ERR: Hardy, Horner
SAC FLY: Horner
LOB: **8**

2001 NY Yankees	AB	R	H	2B	3B	HR	RBI	K	BB
Chuck Knoblauch – LF	4	1	0	0	0	0	0	2	1
Derek Jeter – SS	4	0	0	0	0	0	0	1	0
Paul O'Neill – RF	3	2	1	0	0	1	2	0	0
Bernie Williams – CF	4	0	2	0	0	0	1	2	0
Tino Martinez – 1B	4	0	1	0	0	0	0	1	0
Jorge Posada – C	4	0	0	0	0	0	0	2	0
Shane Spencer – DH	1	0	0	0	0	0	0	0	1
David Justice – DH	1	0	0	0	0	0	0	0	0
Alfonso Soriano – 2B	3	0	1	0	0	0	0	0	0
Scott Brosius – 3B	3	0	1	0	0	0	0	0	0

SB: Knoblauch
SAC FLY: O'Neill
LOB: 3

PITCHING:

AZ All-Time Team	IP	R	ER	H	HR	K	BB
John Denny (W)	6	3	2	4	1	6	2
Bob Milacki	2	0	0	1	0	2	0
Jeremy Affeldt	1	0	0	1	0	1	0

2001 NY Yankees	IP	R	ER	H	HR	K	BB
Andy Pettitte	6	2	2	7	1	6	1
Randy Choate (L)	2/3	5	5	4	0	0	1
Sterling Hitchcock	0	2	2	3	2	0	0
Mike Stanton	1 1/3	0	0	2	0	1	0
Mariano Rivera	1	0	0	2	0	2	0

	1	2	3	4	5	6	7	8	9	R	H	E
AZ All-Time Team	0	0	0	0	0	2	7	0	0	9	18	2
'01 NY Yankees	1	0	0	1	0	1	0	0	0	3	6	0

Game Four: Yankee Stadium

Roger Clemens returned to the bump in an attempt to stave off elimination for the Yankees. Arizona's All-Time Team, however, was determined to end this series.

Billy Hatcher led off the game with a single and later scored on Bob Horner's RBI triple. Paul Konerko followed with a blast into the short porch in right field. The Rocket fanned Tim Salmon and Terry Kennedy to end the inning, but came off the field with the Yanks trailing 3-0.

Taking the mound for Arizona was Camelback alumnus Gary Gentry, who retired the first two batters he faced. Singles by Paul O'Neill and Bernie Williams put runners at the corners and gave Tino Martinez the chance to cut into AZ's lead. The Yankee slugger, however, popped out to second baseman Ian Kinsler to end the inning.

Clemens settled down, shutting out Arizona in the second and third innings. In the bottom of the third, Scott Brosius led off with a grounder to third. Horner mishandled the ball, allowing the New York third baseman to reach first safely. Next came Chuck Knoblauch, who singled to left, giving the Yankees two on with nobody out. Manager Joe Torre called on Derek Jeter to lay down a bunt, which he did perfectly. Now the Yanks had men on second and third with one out, and the heart of order coming up against Gentry.

O'Neill hit a fly ball to right, which Salmon caught. However, it wasn't deep enough to score Brosius. Williams then hit a bouncer toward short. Knoblauch took off running, but the ball clipped him in the leg and deflected back toward second base. The umpire ruled runner's interference and called Knoblauch out. Gentry and the rest of his Arizona teammates breathed a sigh of relief as they emerged unscathed from the situation.

Both Clemens and Gentry spent the middle frames hanging bagels on the board, scattering just a handful of hits. The Yankees threatened again in the bottom of the sixth with two on and two out. David Justice smacked a fly ball to right-centerfield. Hatcher blazed across the outfield grass and made a diving catch to end the inning and the Yankee threat.

In the seventh, Clemens gave up a leadoff single to J.J. Hardy, then moved him to second on a balk. After walking Tom Pagnozzi, the Yankees went to their bullpen, which has had issues throughout the series.

Ramiro Mendoza faced Hatcher first and got him to fly out to center. Kinsler then grounded to short. Jeter got Pagnozzi at second, then Alfonso Soriano spun and threw to first. The hustling Kinsler just beat out the throw to avoid an inning ending double play.

Horner came up next and swung at the first pitch for strike one. Mendoza was just two strikes away from getting out of the inning and keeping the game within reach.

Horner lined the next pitch to left. Knoblauch chased after it, only to watch the ball just clear the fence for a three-run homer. Arizona now led 6-0.

Gentry retired the Yanks in order in the bottom of the seventh. In the top of the eighth, New York brought in Jay Witasick to pitch. Singles by Salmon and Kennedy and a walk to Hank Leiber loaded the bases with nobody out and earned the Yankee reliever a quick exit. On came lefty Mike Stanton, who fanned Hardy. Pagnozzi flew out to left, deep enough to score Salmon and make it 7-0 Arizona. Hatcher then hit a slow roller down the first base line. Martinez and Stanton watched it roll, waiting for the ball to go foul.

It didn't.

Arizona had the bases loaded again with Kinsler up. His patient eye earned him a walk and an RBI, increasing Arizona's lead to 8-0.

Out came Stanton, and in came Mariano Rivera. One of the game's greatest closers gave up a base hit to Horner, who drove in his fifth run of the game. Rivera got Konerko to fly out to center to end the inning.

Gentry proved untouchable in the eighth as he got Jeter to pop out, then struck out O'Neill and Williams. That would prove the end of his night, as Manager Jim Brock went to the bullpen to have Lerrin LaGrow finish it. The ASU standout first faced Martinez, who flew out to left. Next came Jorge Posada, who grounded out to second. That left Justice as the last hope for the Yankees. LaGrow got him swinging for strike three, sealing the deal on a 9-0 Arizona win and a four-game sweep.

AZ All-Time Team	AB	R	H	2B	3B	HR	RBI	K	BB
Billy Hatcher – CF	5	1	2	0	0	0	0	0	0
Ian Kinsler – 2B	4	1	0	0	0	0	1	2	1
George Grantham – 2B (8th)	0	0	0	0	0	0	0	0	0
Bob Horner – 3B	5	2	3	0	1	1	5	1	0
Shea Hillenbrand – 3B (8th)	0	0	0	0	0	0	0	0	0
Paul Konerko – 1B	5	1	2	0	0	1	2	1	0
Tim Salmon – RF	4	1	1	0	0	0	0	1	0
Mickey Hatcher – PH/RF (9th)	1	0	1	0	0	0	0	0	0
Terry Kennedy – DH	5	1	1	0	0	0	0	1	0
Andre Ethier – LF	3	0	1	0	0	0	0	0	0
Hank Leiber – PH/LF (8th)	1	1	0	0	0	0	0	0	1
J.J. Hardy – SS	4	1	2	0	0	0	0	1	0
Tom Pagnozzi – C	1	0	0	0	0	0	1	1	2

ERR: Hardy
SB: Hatcher
SAC FLY: Pagnozzi
LOB: 6

2001 NY Yankees	AB	R	H	2B	3B	HR	RBI	K	BB
Chuck Knoblauch – LF	4	0	1	0	0	0	0	1	0
Derek Jeter – SS	3	0	0	0	0	0	0	0	0
Paul O'Neill – RF	4	0	1	0	0	0	0	1	0
Bernie Williams – CF	4	0	2	0	0	0	0	1	0
Tino Martinez – 1B	4	0	0	0	0	0	0	1	0
Jorge Posada – C	4	0	1	0	0	0	0	1	0
David Justice – DH	4	0	1	0	0	0	0	1	0
Alfonso Soriano – 2B	3	0	0	0	0	0	0	0	0
Scott Brosius – 3B	3	0	0	0	0	0	0	0	0

SAC: Jeter
LOB: 5

PITCHING:

AZ All-Time Team	IP	R	ER	H	HR	K	BB
Gary Gentry (W)	8	0	0	6	0	5	0
Lerrin LaGrow	1	0	0	0	0	1	0

2001 NY Yankees	IP	R	ER	H	HR	K	BB
Roger Clemens (L)	6	4	4	7	1	7	2
Ramiro Mendoza	1	2	2	1	1	0	1
Jay Witasick	0	1	1	1	0	0	0
Mike Stanton	2/3	2	2	1	0	1	1
Mariano Rivera	1 1/3	0	0	2	0	0	0

	1	2	3	4	5	6	7	8	9	R	H	E
AZ All-Time Team	3	0	0	0	0	0	3	3	0	9	13	1
'01 NY Yankees	0	0	0	0	0	0	0	0	0	0	6	0

Arizona's All-Time Baseball Team made pretty easy work of the 2001 Yankees. So how about we up the competition for this next round of games? Since many of the players on this team have been all-stars in their careers, and some *should* have been selected to an all-star team, let's pit them against teams made up of other all-stars. We start with one of the greatest assemblages of star power in baseball history. The first-ever American League All-Star Team from 1933. This is a squad that boasted 12 future Hall of Famers, including two Leftys (Grove and Gomez), Jimmie Foxx, who won the Triple Crown and MVP that year, Tony Lazzeri, Lou Gehrig and Babe Ruth.

ROSTER:

Pitchers:
* Lefty Gomez (NY)
General Crowder (WSH)
Wes Ferrell (CLE)
Lefty Grove (PHL)
Oral Hildebrand (CLE)

Catchers:
* Rick Ferrell (BOS)
Bill Dickey (NY)

Infielders:
* Lou Gehrig (NY)
* Charlie Gehringer (DET)
* Joe Cronin (WSH)
* Jimmy Dykes (CHI)
# Jimmie Foxx (PHL)
# Tony Lazzeri (NY)

Outfielders:
* Ben Chapman (NY)
* Al Simmons (CHI)
* Babe Ruth (NY)
Earl Averill (CLE)
Sammy West (STL)

Hall of Fame
* Starter

1933 AL Leaders: Foxx (Triple Crown, 48 Home Runs, 163 RBIs, .356 and MVP); Crowder and Grove (Wins, 24); Gomez (Strikeouts, 163); Gehrig (Runs, 138); Chapman (Stolen Bases, 27); Cronin (Doubles, 45); Hildebrand (Shutouts, 6)

With a slew of Hall of Famers, including legends like Babe Ruth and Lou Gehrig, it looked like this could be a romp for the 1933 AL All-Stars.

Instead, it wound up being an epic battle between the two clubs.

Arizona starter Gil Heredia found himself in trouble early when he allowed back-to-back singles to Charlie Gehringer and Ruth. That put runners at the corners for Gehrig, who drove in 140 runs in 1933. He flew out to center, but Gehringer was able to score. Al Simmons struck out to end the first inning and Heredia managed to get past some of the game's best hitters with minimal damage.

Lefty Gomez, a 16-game winner for the Yankees in '33, drew the start for the All-Stars. The first batter he faced, Billy Hatcher, singled off him. Manager Jim Brock wasted no time in being aggressive on the basepaths and gave the green light to the speedy outfielder from Williams. AL catcher Rick Ferrell, however, gunned down Hatcher for out number one. Aside from a Bob Horner single, Gomez got through the rest of the inning unscathed.

In the bottom of the second, Andre Ethier walked with one out. J.J. Hardy followed with a single. Next came Tom Pagnozzi, looking to tie the score. He stroked a fly to left field that fell into the glove of Ben Chapman. Heredia grounded out to third to end the inning with Arizona still down 1-0.

Chapman led off the top of the third for the AL with a single. The next two batters, Gehringer and Ruth, both grounded into fielder's choices. Heredia was one out away from getting out of the inning.

Gehrig singled, then Heredia walked Simmons. The All-Stars had the bases loaded with Jimmy Dykes at the plate. With the count 2-1, he scorched a liner off his bat . . .

And into the glove of Horner! Arizona's All-Time Team survived the inning without allowing a run.

To the bottom of the fourth, with the score still 1-0 in favor of the AL. Tim Salmon started the inning by striking out, but Ethier followed with a single. Next came Hardy, who hit a tapper to first. Gehrig charged in to get it, but the only play he could make was to tag out Hardy. Ethier advanced safely to second with two outs. With the bottom of the Arizona order up, the All-Stars looked like they should be able to end the inning with ease.

But Gomez walked Pagnozzi to put two on with two out. The next batter was Heredia, a career .213 hitter. Not bad for a pitcher.

The Nogales native hit a grounder to first. Gehrig easily scooped it up and stepped on the bag for the final out. At the end of four, it was still 1-0 American League.

Neither team scored in the fifth. Simmons led off the top of the sixth against Heredia, who appeared settled in.

That feeling didn't last long. Simmons blasted the ball into the left-center field stands to put the All-Stars up 2-0.

After Arizona failed to score in the bottom of the sixth, Heredia got Chapman to ground out to short to begin the top of the seventh. With the

All-Stars sending up three straight left-handed batters, Brock pulled Heredia and brought in Alex Kellner. He got Gehringer to ground to second for the second out of the inning. Now all Kellner had to do was get the Bambino out to retire the side in order.

Ruth had other plans. He laced the ball into right-center field, bouncing it into the stands for a ground rule double. His Yankee teammate, Gehrig, followed with an RBI single. Simmons then grounded into a fielder's choice to short, but the AL now had a 3-0 lead.

Gomez was pinch-hit for by Earl Averill in the eighth inning. The Cleveland outfielder, who drove in 92 runs in 1933, grounded to second to end the frame. The AL brought in Oral Hildebrand to pitch the bottom of the eighth. A 16-game winner for the Indians and the league leader in shutouts with six, he was the perfect man to get the final six outs and secure the win for the All-Stars.

The first batter he faced was Paul Konerko, who walked. After Salmon popped out to first, Ethier drove the ball to right for a single, advancing Konerko to third. Next was Hardy. Hildebrand ran the count to 1-2, then went with a curveball away. The ball cracked off Hardy's bat, flying high to left field. Chapman gave chase, going back, back . . .

Gone! Chase Field erupted in cheers as Hardy's three-run jack knotted the game at three-all.

To the ninth inning. Bobby Howry started the frame by getting Chapman to fly out to left. With left-handed bats coming up, Brock lifted the Yavapai College alumnus for Jeremy Affeldt. He got Gehringer to ground out to second. Just one more out to go to close out the inning.

Affeldt pitched carefully to Ruth. Too carefully, as the Sultan of Swat walked. Next came Gehrig, who hit a fly ball to left. The inning appeared over.

But Ethier mishandled the ball! Ruth made it to third safely, while Gehrig got to second. The All-Stars had two runners in scoring position and two outs with Simmons, who'd homered earlier, at the plate.

The White Sox outfielder hit a fly ball to center. Hatcher turned on the jets, racing after the ball that was falling fast . . .

And made a shoestring catch to end the AL threat!

Arizona started the bottom of the ninth with Ian Kinsler striking out. Next came Horner, who stroked a double to left-center field. Konerko stepped to the plate with a chance to win the game. That's when manager Connie Mack went to the mound to take out Hildebrand and replace him with General Crowder, who won 24 games for Washington in 1933. He got Konerko to pop out, then snagged a comebacker to the mound and threw out Salmon at first. With the score tied 3-3, both sides headed to extra innings.

Bob Milacki came out of the bullpen as Arizona's sixth pitcher of the night. He set down the All-Stars with little trouble in both the tenth and eleventh innings. Crowder also set down Arizona in order in the same frames.

In the top of the twelfth, Simmons led off with a single. Dykes laid down a bunt in front of the plate. New catcher Terry Kennedy fielded it cleanly and got Dykes at first, but Simmons moved to second, representing the go-ahead run for the AL. Joe Cronin was next, looking for his first hit of the game. Instead, he grounded to third and Simmons was forced to hold at second. Mack decided to send up his other catcher, Bill Dickey, to pinch-hit for Ferrell since the New York backstop had more pop than his counterpart from Boston.

Dickey used his pop to pop out to Kinsler at second to end the inning.

For the bottom of the twelfth, Crowder had to work his way through the heart of the Arizona order. The first batter he faced was Horner, who singled for his fourth hit of the game. Next came Konerko, who was 0-4 with a walk. He watched the first pitch all the way into Dickey's glove for strike one.

The next pitch jumped off his bat into left field. Chapman's replacement, Sammy West, ran after the ball, watching as it carried farther and farther away . . .

And into the stands!

Arms raised, Konerko circled the bases, his walk-off home run giving Arizona the 5-3 victory over the 1933 AL All-Stars.

1933 AL All-Stars

	AB	R	H	2B	3B	HR	RBI	K	BB
Ben Chapman – LF	5	0	1	0	0	0	0	0	0
Sammy West – PH/LF (11th)	1	0	0	0	0	0	0	1	0
Charlie Gehringer – 2B	6	1	2	0	0	0	0	0	0
Babe Ruth – RF	4	1	2	1	0	0	0	0	2
Lou Gehrig – 1B	5	0	2	0	0	0	2	0	0
Al Simmons – CF	5	1	2	0	0	1	1	1	1
Jimmy Dykes –3B	5	0	1	1	0	0	0	1	0
Joe Cronin – SS	6	0	0	0	0	0	0	0	0
Rick Ferrell – C	5	0	1	0	0	0	0	1	0
Bill Dickey – PH/C (12th)	1	0	0	0	0	0	0	0	0
Lefty Gomez – P	3	0	0	0	0	0	0	1	0
Earl Averill – PH (8th)	1	0	0	0	0	0	0	0	0
Oral Hildebrand – P (8th)	0	0	0	0	0	0	0	0	0
General Crowder – P (9th)	1	0	0	0	0	0	0	0	0

SAC: Dykes
SAC FLY: Gehrig
ERR: Gehringer
LOB: 11

AZ All-Time Team

	AB	R	H	2B	3B	HR	RBI	K	BB
Billy Hatcher – CF	6	0	1	0	0	0	0	0	0
Ian Kinsler – 2B	6	0	1	0	0	0	0	2	0
Bob Horner – 3B	5	1	4	1	0	0	0	0	1
Paul Konerko – 1B	5	2	1	0	0	1	2	0	1
Tim Salmon – RF	5	0	1	0	0	0	0	1	0
Andre Ethier – LF	3	1	2	0	0	0	0	0	0
J.J. Hardy – SS	5	1	2	0	0	1	3	0	0
Tom Pagnozzi – C	3	0	0	0	0	0	0	1	1
Terry Kennedy – PH/C (10th)	1	0	0	0	0	0	0	1	0
Gil Heredia – P	2	0	0	0	0	0	0	0	0
Alex Kellner – P (7th)	0	0	0	0	0	0	0	0	0
Shea Hillenbrand – PH (7th)	1	0	0	0	0	0	0	0	0
Lerrin LaGrow – P (8th)	0	0	0	0	0	0	0	0	0
George Grantham – PH (8th)	1	0	0	0	0	0	0	0	0
Bobby Howry – P (9th)	0	0	0	0	0	0	0	0	0
Jeremy Affeldt – P (9th)	0	0	0	0	0	0	0	0	0
Bob Milacki – P (10th)	1	0	0	0	0	0	0	0	0

CS: B. Hatcher
SAC: Ethier
ERR: Horner, Ethier, Konerko
LOB: 9

PITCHING:

1933 AL All-Stars	IP	R	ER	H	HR	K	BB
Lefty Gomez	7	0	0	7	0	4	3
Oral Hildebrand	1	3	3	3	1	1	1
General Crowder (L)	3	2	2	3	1	2	0

AZ All-Time Team	IP	R	ER	H	HR	K	BB
Gil Heredia	6 1/3	2	2	7	1	3	2
Alex Kellner	2/3	1	1	2	0	0	0
Lerrin LaGrow	1	0	0	0	0	0	0
Bobby Howry	1/3	0	0	0	0	0	0
Jeremy Affeldt	2/3	0	0	0	0	0	0
Bob Milacki (W)	3	0	0	2	0	2	0

	1	2	3	4	5	6	7	8	9	10	11	12	R	H	E
1933 AL All-Stars	1	0	0	0	0	1	1	0	0	0	0	0	3	11	1
AZ All-Time Team	0	0	0	0	0	0	0	3	0	0	0	2	5	11	3

The next team of superstars to challenge Arizona's All-Time Team is the 1955 National League All-Star Team. Not only is this a squad with nine Hall of Famers, including Hank Aaron, Ernie Banks, Willie and the Duke – no Mickey, since he was in the American League – this is also one of the most explosive line-ups ever assembled for a Mid-Summer Classic. The players on the '55 All-Star Team hit a combined 545 home runs that year. Even the pitchers were no slouches at the plate, as the seven hurlers on the roster hit a total of 14 homers, seven of them by Brooklyn's Don Newcombe. When it came to their performances on the mound, the NL starter, Hall of Famer Robin Roberts, led the league in wins (23), complete games (26) and innings pitched (305). "Newk" was a 20-game winner, the Redlegs Joe Nuxhall was number one in shutouts with five, and despite losing 20 games, the Cubs Sam Jones won the strikeout crown with 198.

Let's see if Arizona is up to this challenge.

ROSTER:

Pitchers:
* Robin Roberts (PHL)
Harvey Haddix (STL)
Don Newcombe (BRO)
Sam Jones (CHI)
Joe Nuxhall (CIN)
Gene Conley (MIL)
Luis Arroyo (STL)

Catchers:
* Del Crandall (MIL)
Smoky Burgess (CIN)
Stan Lopata (PHL)
Roy Campanella (BRO)

INFIELDERS:
* Ted Kluszewski (CIN)
# * Red Schoendienst (STL)
# * Ernie Banks (CHI)
# * Eddie Mathews (MIL)
Gil Hodges (BRO)
Stan Musial (STL)
Gene Baker (CHI)
Johnny Logan (MIL)
Randy Jackson (CHI)

OUTFIELDERS:
*Del Ennis (PHL)
* Duke Snider (BRO)
* Don Mueller (NY)
# Hank Aaron (MIL)
# Willie Mays (NY)
Frank Thomas (PIT)

* Starter
# Hall of Fame

1955 NL Leaders: Mays (51 home runs, .659 SLG, 382 total bases and tied with 13 triples); Snider (136 RBIs and 126 runs); Kluszewski (192 hits); Logan and Aaron (37 doubles); Roberts (23 wins, 26 complete games and 305 innings pitched); Jones (198 strikeouts); Nuxhall (5 complete games); Campanella (MVP, .325, 32 HR, 107 RBIs)

One of the oldest adages in baseball is, "Good pitching beats good hitting." The 1955 NL All-Star Team definitely had some good hitters, and Arizona's All-Time Team countered with its ace, Jim Palmer. Not to be outdone, The NL went with an ace of their own, Robin Roberts.

The Phillies top pitcher of the 1950s set down the side in order for the first three innings at Milwaukee's County Stadium. Palmer got out of the first two innings relatively unscathed, allowing a single to Duke Snider and a walk to Ted Kluszewski. After fanning Del Crandall to start the bottom of the third, Roberts followed with a pop up to third base that Bob Horner misjudged. He reached for it, but the ball bounced off his glove and Roberts reached first safely. Red Schoendienst also reached first safely when he singled, moving Roberts to third. Up came Del Ennis, who flied out to Andre Ethier in left. Roberts scored easily, giving the NL a 1-0 lead. Snider looked to keep the inning going with a grounder up the middle, but J.J. Hardy fielded it and stepped on the bag to end the inning.

Billy Hatcher started the top of the fourth for Arizona with a groundout to short. Next was George Grantham, who got the start at second to give Arizona another left-handed bat. The move by skipper Jim Brock paid off as the Flagstaff product doubled to the opposite field. Horner then came to the plate, looking to redeem himself after his error that led to an NL run.

He laced the ball to left-center field. Grantham rounded third and slid into home to knot the score 1-1. Paul Konerko followed, with a chance to give Arizona the lead. Instead, he hit a roller to first that Kluszewski fielded and took to the bag himself. Horner advanced to third with Tim Salmon at bat. Ahead in the count 1-2, Roberts brought the heat. Salmon took a big hack . . .

For strike three.

The National League looked to regain the lead in the bottom of the fourth as Kluszewski led off with a walk. Next came Eddie Mathews, who grounded to second for a fielder's choice. With one on and one out, Don Mueller, one of the New York Giants top hitters in 1955 with a .306 average, stepped into the batter's box. He bounced the ball back to Palmer, who spun and threw to second for one. Hardy gunned the ball to first and got Mueller for the inning ending double play. After four, the score in Milwaukee was still 1-1.

Arizona began the fifth inning with a single by Terry Kennedy, who got the start behind the plate to give the team another lefty in the line-up. Roberts, however, struck out Ethier and retired Hardy and Palmer on groundouts to end the inning.

The All-Stars also led off their portion of fifth inning with a single, this one from "Mr. Cub" Ernie Banks. Manager Leo Durocher went to his bench and brought in Brooklyn catcher Roy Campanella to pinch-hit for Crandall. The three-time league MVP hit a bouncer up the middle that was fielded by Hardy, who flipped it to Grantham for the force at second.

Next came Roberts. Arizona was looking for the bunt, and that's exactly what the Phillies ace did. But he bunted the ball to the mound. Palmer grabbed it and threw to second to get the runner. Hardy fired the ball to first and nailed Roberts for another inning ending double play.

With five innings in the books, the NL and Arizona remained tied 1-1.

In the top of the sixth, Roberts got Billy Hatcher to fly out to right. Grantham delivered his second hit of the day, a single to right. Horner followed with a flyout to center, then Konerko grounded to Banks, who tossed the ball to Schoendienst at second for the final out.

The NL second sacker led off the bottom of the frame by popping out to the catcher Kennedy. Up to the plate came Ennis. The second pitch he saw from Palmer he blasted into the left field stands for a home run. The National League was back on top 2-1. A pair of flyouts sandwiched between a Kluszewski single ended the inning.

Salmon led off the top of the seventh for Arizona by flying out to Snider in center. Kennedy came to the plate next and worked a walk. Ethier followed with a single that put runners at the corners with one out and Hardy at bat. The Arizona shortstop hit a sharp grounder to Mathews. Ethier made it to second, but Kennedy was stuck at third. Mathews threw to first to get Hardy for out number two. That brought up Palmer, with a chance to help his own cause. He hit a bouncing ball that looked like it would go into left for a base hit. But the ball struck Ethier in the leg for an automatic out. Roberts preserved a 2-1 lead for the NL All-Stars.

Palmer got through the bottom of the seventh with relative ease. Arizona faced a new pitcher in the top of the eighth, Brooklyn's Don Newcombe. Hatcher led off the inning by striking out for the second time in the game. Grantham followed with a walk. Horner grounded deep in the hole at second, but the only play Schoendienst had was to first. There were two down with a man on second and Konerko at the plate.

The former Chaparral Firebird hit a moonshot to right-center field. Both Snider and Mueller could only watch as it landed near the scoreboard. Arizona led for the first time in the game 3-2.

Salmon followed that up with a single, and it looked like Arizona had "Newk" on the ropes. Next up was Kennedy, who smacked a liner toward right field. Schoendienst made a diving catch to bring the inning to a close.

Palmer set down the All-Stars in the bottom of the eighth with little trouble. In the top of the ninth, Newcombe gave up a leadoff single to Ethier. Brock then turned to his bench for a parade of pinch-hitters to try and up Arizona's lead. First was Solly Hemus, in for Hardy. He hit a grounder to short that Banks threw to second to force out Ethier. Next came Shea Hillenbrand, pinch-hitting for Palmer. Newcombe struck him out. Hatcher, suffering through an 0-4 game, was subbed out for Hank Leiber. He popped out to the catcher to end the inning.

Mike MacDougal came on in the ninth to get the save. Up first for the NL was Mathews. He walked. Next was Stan "The Man" Musial, who replaced Mueller in the seventh. He also walked. MacDougal found himself in a bind. The All-Stars had two men on and nobody out with Banks at the plate. He stroked the ball to short. Hemus made a diving stab for it, but the ball ticked off his webbing and rolled into left field. Ethier charged in to get it as Mathews tore around third, heading home with the tying run. Ethier came up throwing to the plate . . .

And nailed Mathews! Arizona preserved its lead, but the NL had runners on first and second with one out and Campanella at bat. The Brooklyn catcher struck out. MacDougal had one more out to get to lock down a win for Arizona. He just had to get through the NL's pinch-hitter.

That pinch-hitter was the up and coming Hank Aaron, who batted .280 with 13 home runs and 69 RBIs for Milwaukee in his rookie year of 1954. With a 1-1 count, Aaron laced the ball into left field. Musial came round from second to score the tying run.

The save blown, Brock lifted his closer in favor of Jeremy Affeldt. He got Schoendienst to ground out to end the inning with the score 3-3.

Onto extras. New All-Star pitcher Joe Nuxhall retired Grantham and Horner on back-to-back groundouts before walking Konerko. That free pass wouldn't hurt the Cincinnati pitcher as he fanned Salmon to wrap up the inning. Affeldt set down the NL 1-2-3 in the bottom of the frame. The score remained knotted at three as both sides headed into the eleventh inning.

Kennedy led off with a base hit, then advanced to second on a slow roller to first. Hemus popped out to third for out number two. Brock sent Mickey Hatcher to bat for Affeldt. He hit a fly ball to left-center field. Both Ennis and Snider gave chase . . .

And the ball dropped between them! Kennedy rounded third and came home with the go-ahead run.

Next up was Leiber. He smacked a single to left to plate Hatcher for the insurance run. After a walk to Grantham, Nuxhall was lifted for Gene Conley, who got Horner to ground out the third. The inning ended with Arizona up 5-3.

Bobby Howry came on to pitch the bottom of the eleventh, and gave up a leadoff single to Mathews with Musial up. He struck out "The Man," but wasn't out of the woods yet. Next up was Banks. The NL shortstop hit a bouncer to short. Hemus snagged it and threw to second for one out. Grantham pivoted and fired to first. Konerko caught it for the final out, giving Arizona the 5-3 win over one of the most potent line-ups ever assembled.

AZ All-Time Team	AB	R	H	2B	3B	HR	RBI	K	BB
Billy Hatcher – CF	4	0	0	0	0	0	0	2	0
Hank Leiber – PH/CF (9th)	2	1	1	0	0	0	1	0	0
George Grantham – 2B	4	2	2	1	0	0	0	1	2
Bob Horner – 3B	6	0	1	1	0	0	1	0	0
Paul Konerko – 1B	4	1	1	0	0	1	2	1	1
Tim Salmon – RF	5	0	1	0	0	0	0	1	0
Terry Kennedy – C	4	1	2	0	0	0	0	0	1
Andre Ethier – LF	5	0	1	0	0	0	0	1	0
J.J. Hardy – SS	3	0	0	0	0	0	0	0	0
Solly Hemus – PH/SS (9th)	2	0	0	0	0	0	0	0	0
Jim Palmer – P	3	0	0	0	0	0	0	0	0
Shea Hillenbrand – PH (9th)	1	0	0	0	0	0	0	0	1
Mike MacDougal – P (9th)	0	0	0	0	0	0	0	0	0
Jeremy Affeldt – P (9th)	0	0	0	0	0	0	0	0	0
Mickey Hatcher – PH (11th)	1	1	1	1	0	0	1	0	0

ERR: Horner
LOB: 6

1955 NL All-Stars	AB	R	H	2B	3B	HR	RBI	K	BB
Red Schoendienst – 2B	5	0	1	0	0	0	0	1	0
Del Ennis – LF	4	1	2	0	0	1	2	1	0
Duke Snider – CF	5	0	1	0	0	0	0	0	0
Ted Kluszewski – 1B	3	0	1	0	0	0	0	1	1
Gil Hodges – PH/1B (10th)	1	0	0	0	0	0	0	0	0
Eddie Mathews – 3B	3	0	1	0	0	0	0	0	2
Don Mueller – RF	2	0	0	0	0	0	0	0	0
Stan Musial – PH/RF (7th)	2	1	0	0	0	0	0	1	1
Ernie Banks – SS	5	0	2	0	0	0	0	1	0
Del Crandall – C	1	0	0	0	0	0	0	1	0
Roy Campanella – PH/C (5th)	2	0	0	0	0	0	0	1	1
Robin Roberts – P	2	1	0	0	0	0	0	0	0
Willie Mays – PH (7th)	1	0	0	0	0	0	0	0	0
Don Newcombe – P (8th)	0	0	0	0	0	0	0	0	0
Hank Aaron – PH (9th)	1	0	1	0	0	0	1	0	0
Joe Nuxhall – P (10th)	0	0	0	0	0	0	0	0	0
Gene Conley – P (11th)	0	0	0	0	0	0	0	0	0

SAC FLY: Ennis
LOB: 5

PITCHING:

AZ All-Time Team	IP	R	ER	H	HR	K	BB
Jim Palmer	8	2	1	6	1	5	3
Mike MacDougal (BS)	2/3	1	1	1	0	0	2
Jeremy Affeldt (W)	1 1/3	0	0	0	0	0	0
Bobby Howry (SV)	1	0	0	1	0	1	0

1955 NL All-Stars	IP	R	ER	H	HR	K	BB
Robin Roberts	7	1	1	5	0	5	1
Don Newcombe	2	2	2	3	1	2	0
Joe Nuxhall (L)	1 1/3	2	2	3	0	1	1
Gene Conley	1/3	0	0	0	0	0	0

	1	2	3	4	5	6	7	8	9	10	11	R	H	E
AZ All-Time Team	0	0	0	1	0	0	0	2	0	0	2	5	11	1
1955 NL All-Stars	0	0	1	0	0	1	0	0	1	0	0	3	8	0

Two all-star teams have gone down in defeat to Arizona's All-Time Team. So, in the words of a famous pro wrestler from years ago, "Who's next?"

That would be the 1965 National League All-Star Team, featuring some of the top pitchers of the decade. Four of them are enshrined in Cooperstown. Juan Marichal, Sandy Koufax, Bob Gibson and Don Drysdale. In 1965, those four combined for 91 wins and 1,102 strikeouts. But they weren't the only outstanding pitchers on this roster. Sammy Ellis and Jim Maloney were 20-game winners for the Cincinnati Reds, while Bob Veale was second in the league behind Koufax in strikeouts with 276. Koufax, by the way, was far ahead of Veale for the NL lead in K's with 382.

While the 1960s was the decade where pitchers shined, there were still plenty of big bats to go around. The '65 All-Stars featured sluggers like Willie Mays, Hank Aaron, Frank Robinson and Johnny Callison. Even though they were not blessed with a lot of power, two of the best table-setters of the decade, Pete Rose and Maury Wills, were part of the starting line-up.

Time to see if Arizona can take down another team of baseball's best.

ROSTER

Pitchers:
\# * Juan Marichal (SF)
\# Don Drysdale (LA)
\# Sandy Koufax (LA)
\# Bob Gibson (STL)
Bob Veale (PIT)
Jim Maloney (CIN)
Turk Farrell (HOU)
Sammy Ellis (CIN)

Catchers:
* Joe Torre (MIL)
Johnny Edwards (CIN)

Infielders:
\# * Ernie Banks (CHI)
* Pete Rose (CIN)
* Maury Wills (LA)
* Dick Allen (PHL)
Ed Kranepool (NY)
Cookie Rojas (PHL)
Leo Cardenas (CIN)
\# Ron Santo (CHI)

Outfielders:
\# * Willie Stargell (PIT)
\# * Willie Mays (SF)
\# * Hank Aaron (MIL)
\# Roberto Clemente (PIT)
Johnny Callison (PHL)
\# Frank Robinson (CIN)
\# Billy Williams (CHI)

\# Hall of Fame
* Starter

1965 League Leaders: Mays (MVP, 52 home runs, .645 slugging percentage, .398 on-base percentage), Clemente (.329 average), Aaron (40 doubles), Callison (16 triples), Wills (94 stolen bases), Rose (209 hits), Koufax (26 wins, 382 strikeouts, 2.04 ERA, 27 complete games, 335 innings pitched and Cy Young), Marichal (10 shutouts).

The pitchers took center stage at Metropolitan Stadium in Bloomington, Minnesota, at least for the early part of the game. Arizona's Curt Schilling set the side down in order in each of the first three innings. NL starter Juan Marichal was almost as sharp, as he faced one over the minimum during that stretch.

Just when it looked like Schilling was in control, Willie Mays led off the All-Stars' half of the fourth inning with blast into the right field stands. Hank Aaron followed with a home run over the right-center field fence to put the '65 NL All-Stars on top 2-0.

Willie Stargell singled to right, and all the makings of a big inning seemed to be falling into place. The next batter for the NL was power-hitting third baseman Dick Allen. He took a big hack at Schilling's first pitch . . . and missed. Allen fell behind in the count 1-2 when Schilling threw a fastball away. The Philadelphia slugger swung . . . and missed!

Next came another power threat, Braves catcher Joe Torre, who hit 27 home runs and drove in 80 runs in 1965. He hit a bouncer to the left side, which J.J. Hardy easily fielded to begin the 6-4-3 inning ending double play.

The top of the fifth started with Shea Hillenbrand striking out. That brought up Andre Ethier, who singled to right. Next was J.J. Hardy, looking to get a rally going. He hit a slow roller toward short. Maury Wills fielded the ball and threw to second for one out, but Pete Rose was unable to turn the double play. Arizona still had a runner on first, but now with two outs and Tom Pagnozzi up. He grounded out to third to conclude the inning.

After Ernie Banks grounded to short to start the sixth, Rose smacked the ball to right-centerfield. He flew around the bases as the ball rolled all the way to the wall and wound up with a triple. Wills stepped into the batter's box, looking to extend the NL lead. He hit a chopper toward second. Kinsler fielded it deep in the hole, and had no chance to get Rose coming home. He threw to first to get Wills, whose groundout gave the All-Stars a 3-0 lead.

Marichal ended the inning with a groundout to short, then headed back to the mound to try and keep his shutout alive. His first batter was Schilling, who hit a slow roller down the third base line. Allen charged in to get it and threw to first, but Schilling just beat the throw. Billy Hatcher came up next and nearly duplicated Schilling's at-bat by also hitting a slow roller, this one down the first base line. Banks's only play was to tag Hatcher, allowing Schilling to advance to second. It was the first time in the game Arizona had a runner in scoring position. It was now up to Kinsler to make the most of it.

On a 1-1 count, Marichal brought the heat. Kinsler belted it into the left field bleachers for a two-run shot. Tim Salmon and Paul Konerko followed with a strikeout and a groundout respectively, but Arizona was back in the game, down 3-2.

After Mays flew out to center to begin the bottom of the sixth, Aaron singled. That brought up Stargell, who bounced it to first. Konerko stepped on the bag for one, then threw to second for the double play.

Marichal took the hill with renewed determination in the top of the seventh. He fanned Hillenbrand, Ethier and Hardy, the second time the "Dominican Dandy" struck out the side. The bottom of the seventh looked to be no problem for Schilling. He got pinch-hitter Ron Santo to fly out to right, then got Torre to ground out to short. That brought up Banks, who was 0-2 in the game. He smacked a line drive to left. Ethier gave chase, but pulled up short of the warning track and watched it sail over the fence. The NL doubled its lead to 4-2.

Marichal set down the side in order in the top of the eighth. In the bottom of the frame, Lerrin LaGrow took over for Schilling. The first batter he faced was Wills, who tripled to center field. With a great chance to extend their lead, Manager Gene Mauch sent Johnny Callison up to pinch-hit for Marichal. The Phillies outfielder, who had 32 homers and 101 RBIs in 1965, hit a comebacker to the mound. Wills was stuck at third while LeGrow easily threw out Callison.

Mays was next. The "Say Hey Kid" bounced it to Hillenbrand at third. Again, Wills was forced to hold as Mays was thrown out. That put it on Aaron's shoulders to get the run in.

On the second pitch he saw from LaGrow, "Hammerin' Hank" ripped a liner down the third base line . . . and right into Hillenbrand's glove. Inning over.

Arizona was down to its last at-bat and had another tough pitcher to face. This time it was 20-game winner Bob Gibson. He got Kinsler to fly out to center for out number one. Salmon followed with a grounder to short . . . that Wills booted. The Grand Canyon University product was safe at first, and hope was alive for Arizona.

Konerko came up, then promptly sat down as Gibson struck him out. It all came down to pinch-hitter Solly Hemus. He bounced the ball to second. Rose fielded it cleanly and threw to defensive replacement Ed Kranepool at first for the final out. The 1965 NL All-Stars got the win 4-2 and handed Arizona's All-Time Team its first loss.

AZ All-Time Team

AZ All-Time Team	AB	R	H	2B	3B	HR	RBI	K	BB
Billy Hatcher – CF	4	0	0	0	0	0	0	1	0
Ian Kinsler – 2B	4	1	2	0	0	1	2	0	0
Tim Salmon – RF	4	0	1	0	0	0	0	1	0
Paul Konerko – 1B	4	0	0	0	0	0	0	2	0
Shea Hillenbrand – 3B	3	0	0	0	0	0	0	3	0
Solly Hemus – PH (9th)	1	0	0	0	0	0	0	0	0
Andre Ethier – RF	3	0	1	0	0	0	0	2	0
J.J. Hardy – SS	3	0	0	0	0	0	0	2	0
Tom Pagnozzi – C	3	0	0	0	0	0	0	1	0
Curt Schilling – P	2	1	1	0	0	0	0	0	0
George Grantham – PH (8th)	1	0	0	0	0	0	0	0	0
Lerrin LaGroaw – P (9th)	0	0	0	0	0	0	0	0	0

LOB: 3

1965 NL All-Stars

1965 NL All-Stars	AB	R	H	2B	3B	HR	RBI	K	BB
Willie Mays – CF	4	1	1	0	0	1	1	1	0
Hank Aaron – RF	4	1	2	0	0	1	1	0	0
Willie Stargell – LF	3	0	1	0	0	0	0	0	0
Frank Robinson – LF (9th)	0	0	0	0	0	0	0	0	0
Dick Allen – 3B	2	0	0	0	0	0	0	2	0
Ron Santo – PH/3B (7th)	1	0	0	0	0	0	0	0	0
Joe Torre – C	3	0	0	0	0	0	0	0	0
Ernie Banks – 1B	3	1	1	0	0	1	1	0	0
Ed Kranepool – 1B (9th)	0	0	0	0	0	0	0	0	0
Pete Rose – 2B	3	1	1	0	1	0	0	0	0
Maury Wills – SS	3	0	1	0	1	0	1	0	0
Juan Marichal – P	2	0	0	0	0	0	0	0	0
Johnny Callison – PH (8th)	1	0	0	0	0	0	0	0	0
Bob Gibson – P (9th)	0	0	0	0	0	0	0	0	0

ERR: Wills
LOB: 1

PITCHING:

AZ All-Time Team	IP	R	ER	H	HR	K	BB
Curt Schilling (L)	7	4	4	6	3	3	0
Lerrin LaGrow	1	0	0	1	0	0	0

1965 NL All-Stars	IP	R	ER	H	HR	K	BB
Juan Marichal (W)	8	2	2	5	1	11	0
Bob Gibson (SV)	1	0	0	0	0	1	0

	1	2	3	4	5	6	7	8	9	R	H	E
AZ All-Time Team	0	0	0	0	0	2	0	0	0	2	5	0
1965 NL All-Stars	0	0	0	2	1	0	1	0	X	4	7	1

They went up against three of the best All-Star teams ever assembled and came away with two wins. A very good showing by Arizona's All-Time Baseball Team. But how would they fare against a different collection of star players? What if Arizona took on a squad comprised entirely of American League Rookie of the Year Award winners?

Let's find out.

ROSTER
(Team/Award Year/Stats)

PITCHERS:

Gary Peters *(CHI/1963/19-8, 2.33, 189 K)*
Bob Grim *(NY/1954/20-6, 3.26, 108 K)*
Mark Fidrych *(DET/1976/19-9, 2.34, 97 K)*
Herb Score *(CLE/1955/16-10, 2.85, 245 K)*
Justin Verlander *(DET/2006/17-9, 3.63, 124 K)*
Dave Righetti *(NY/1981/8-4, 2.05, 89 K)*
Gregg Olson *(BAL/1989/5-2, 27 SV, 1.69, 90 K)*
Huston Street *(OAK/2005/5-1, 23 SV, 1.71, 72 K)*
Andrew Bailey *(OAK/2009/6-3, 26 SV, 1.84, 91K)*
Neftali Feliz *(TEX/2010/4-3, 40 SV, 2.73, 71K)*

CATCHERS:

Carlton Fisk *(BOS/1972/.293, 22 HR, 61 RBI, Gold Glove)*
Thurman Munson *(NY/1970/.302, 6 HR, 53 RBI)*

INFIELDERS:

Walt Dropo *(BOS/1950/.322, 34 HR, 144 RBI)*
Dustin Pedroia *(BOS/2007/.317, 8 HR, 50 RBI)*
Derek Jeter *(NY/1996/.314, 10 HR, 78 RBI, 104 R)*
Cal Ripken, Jr. *(BAL/1982/.264, 28 HR, 93 RBI)*
Mark McGuire *(OAK/1987/.289, 49 HR, 118 RBI)*
Rod Carew *(MIN/1967/.292, 8 HR, 51 RBI)*
Evan Longoria *(TB/2008/.272, 27 HR, 85 RBI)*
Tony Kubek *(NY/1957/.297, 3 HR, 39 RBI)*

OUTFIELDERS:

Mike Trout *(LA/2012/.326, 30 HR, 83 RBI, 49 SB, 129 R)*
Fred Lynn *(BOS/1975/.331, 21 HR, 105 RBI, 103 R, 47 2B, MVP, Gold Glove)*
Ichiro Suzuki *(SEA/2001/.350, 8 HR, 69 RBI, 56 SB, MVP, Gold Glove)*
Tony Oliva *(MIN/1964/.323, 32 HR, 94 RBI, 109 R, 43 2B)*
Tommie Agee *(CHI/1966/.273, 22 HR, 86 RBI, 44 SB, Gold Glove)*

The way this game began, it looked like it would be a good day for the offense, and a not-so good day for the pitchers. 1983 Cy Young winner John Denny toed the rubber for Arizona as a collection of American League Rookies of the Year invaded Chase Field. The first man he faced was one of the best hitters of the 2000s. Ichiro Suzuki, who hit .350 in his rookie year of 2001.

Denny promptly struck him out.

Following Ichiro was Dustin Pedroia, who hit a routine grounder to shortstop. J.J. Hardy bent down to snag it, but the ball rolled between his legs and into left field. Pedroia reached first safely on the error. Mike Trout then bounced one toward right field. Ian Kinsler ranged to his left and got the out at first, but Pedroia advanced to second. Denny was one out away from ending the inning, but had to get through Walt Dropo, who led the AL in RBIs with 144 in his 1950 rookie campaign. The Boston first baseman hit a fly ball to deep center field. Billy Hatcher got on his horse, going back, back . . .

The ball struck the wall just under the Chase Field scoreboard for a two-run home run.

Denny fanned Carlton Fisk for the third out, but Arizona was down early to the American League rookies 2-0.

Billy Hatcher led off the bottom of the first for Arizona by grounding out to short. Next came Kinsler, who singled off Rookie starter Gary Peters. He was followed by Horner, who stroked the ball into left field. It took one bounce into the stands for a ground rule double. Arizona had runners on second and third with one out, and slugger Paul Konerko up.

Peters got him swinging for strike three. Now he had to get Tim Salmon out to end the inning.

The Greenway grad hit a fly ball to left. It arced toward the line . . . and hit the ground fair with inches to spare. Kinsler and Horner sprinted across the plate to tie the game at two, while Salmon took second. Next came Andre Ethier, who hit a roller down the third base line. Cal Ripken, Jr. charged in and scooped up the ball, then bobbled it as he tried to throw. Arizona had runners at first and third with two down and Hardy coming to bat, with a chance to redeem himself after that costly error in the top of the inning.

He lined a single to left, driving in Salmon to give Arizona the 3-2 lead.

Peters got Tom Pagnozzi to hit into a 5-4 fielder's choice to end a very rocky first inning.

After Ripken flied out to start the second inning, Fred Lynn doubled. Denny struck out Derek Jeter, then faced Peters, a very good hitting pitcher who batted .259 with three homers and 12 RBIs in his rookie year of 1963.

Peters grounded back to the mound, but Denny mishandled the ball and everyone was safe. That brought Ichiro to the plate. He smacked a single to left. Lynn crossed the plate to tie the game at three. Pedroia grounded into a fielder's choice for out number three.

Denny helped his own cause in the bottom of the second, leading off with a single. That brought up Hatcher, who popped out trying to bunt. Kinsler also tried to lay down a bunt, but missed just as Denny took off for second. Fisk gunned down the pitcher, then Peters finished off Kinsler with a strikeout.

Denny found himself in trouble again in the third. Trout led off with a ground rule double, then moved to third on a Dropo groundout to second. Fisk then hit a sharp grounder down the third base line. Horner snagged it, looked back Trout at third, then threw to first for the out. Ripken struck out for the final out.

The bottom of the third started with back-to-back singles by Horner and Konerko. That ended the day for Peters, who was replaced by one of the most eccentric pitchers in baseball history, 1976 Rookie of the Year Mark Fidrych. The first batter "The Bird" faced, Tim Salmon, singled to left to drive in Horner for the go-ahead run. Ethier struck out, but Hardy singled to load the bases for Pagnozzi. Arizona's catcher flew out to center field. Konerko took off from third as Lynn threw to home. The ball bounced once, then twice, then into the glove of Fisk. He reached down to tag the sliding Konerko.

Out! Fidrych got out of a one-out, bases loaded jam, but the AL Rookies now trailed 4-3 after three innings.

Lynn singled to lead off the top of the fourth, but never advanced past first base. Jeter popped out attempting to bunt, Fidrych flew out to right and Ichiro struck out. The bottom of the fourth started with Denny grounding out to third. Hatcher then struck out, which brought up Kinsler. The second baseman smashed the ball into the left field stands for a solo home run, increasing Arizona's lead to 5-3. Horner followed with a single, but Fidrych prevented further damage by getting Konerko to flyout to center.

The fifth and sixth innings passed with relative quiet for both sides. Denny faced four batters in both innings, giving up singles to Dropo and Jeter, but shutting out the Rookies. Fidrych set down the side in order in both frames.

The seventh inning, however, was anything but quiet.

Alex Kellner relieved Denny and gave up a leadoff single to Ichiro, who promptly stole second. After Pedroia flew out to left, Trout laced a double to center. Ichiro scored to cut Arizona's lead to one. Manager Jim Brock was quick with the hook on Kellner, replacing him with Bob Milacki. The first batter he faced, Dropo, popped out to short. Fisk came to the plate next and lined a single into left-center field. That brought Trout home to tie the score at five. The AL Rookies' rally ended when Ripken grounded back to the mound.

Fidrych set down the side in order in the bottom of the seventh and the bottom of the eighth. Milacki also had a 1-2-3 inning in the top of the eighth.

That set the stage for drama in the ninth inning.

After Ichiro led off with a groundout to second, Pedroia and Trout hit back-to-back singles. The Rookies had two on with one out and the heart of the order due up.

Dropo hit a slow roller down the first base line. Konerko picked it up and put the tag on Dropo, but Trout and Pedroia advanced to second and third respectively. Up came Fisk, looking to put the Rookies ahead again.

Milacki got him swinging for strike three. The score remained tied 5-5 going into the bottom of the ninth.

As Fidrych took the mound for his seventh inning of work, Brock went to his bench. Terry Kennedy pinch hit for Pagnozzi and led off with a single, ending "The Bird's" streak of 13 batters in a row retired. Mickey Hatcher then pinch-hit for Milacki. Fidrych delivered the first two pitches for strikes. The next pitch was a curve.

Hatcher smacked it into left-center field. The ball bounced over the wall for a ground rule double. Arizona had runners on second and third with nobody out.

That brought the other Hatcher, Billy, to the plate. The former Yavapai College standout was 0 for his last 12 at bats. This gave him the perfect opportunity to break out of the slump.

The ball jumped off his bat to the right side of the infield. It hit the grass and trickled toward second. Pedroia hustled for it and picked it up with his bare hand. He looked up just in time to see Kennedy cross the plate with the winning run, final score Arizona 6, AL Rookies 5.

AL Rookies of the Year	AB	R	H	2B	3B	HR	RBI	K	BB
Ichiro Suzuki – RF	5	1	2	0	0	0	0	2	0
Dustin Pedroia – 2B	5	1	1	0	0	0	0	0	0
Mike Trout – LF	5	1	3	2	0	0	1	0	0
Walt Dropo – 1B	5	1	2	0	0	1	2	0	0
Carlton Fisk – C	5	0	1	0	0	0	1	2	0
Cal Ripken, Jr. – 3B	4	0	0	0	0	0	0	1	0
Fred Lynn – CF	4	1	2	1	0	0	0	0	0
Derek Jeter – SS	4	0	1	0	0	0	0	1	0
Gary Peters – P	1	0	0	0	0	0	0	0	0
Mark Fidrych – P (3rd)	3	0	0	0	0	0	0	0	0

SB: Ichiro
ERR: Ripken, Jr.
LOB: 8

AZ All-Time Team	AB	R	H	2B	3B	HR	RBI	K	BB
Billy Hatcher – CF	5	0	1	0	0	0	1	1	0
Ian Kinsler – 2B	4	2	2	0	0	1	1	1	0
Bob Horner – 3B	4	2	3	1	0	0	0	0	0
Paul Konerko – 1B	4	0	1	0	0	0	0	1	0
Tim Salmon – RF	4	1	2	0	0	0	2	0	0
Andre Ethier – LF	4	0	0	0	0	0	0	1	0
J.J. Hardy – SS	4	0	2	0	0	0	0	1	0
Tom Pagnozzi – C	3	0	0	0	0	0	0	0	0
Terry Kennedy – PH (9th)	1	1	1	0	0	0	0	0	0
John Denny – P	2	0	1	0	0	0	0	0	0
George Grantham – PH (6th)	1	0	0	0	0	0	0	0	0
Alex Kellner – P (7th)	0	0	0	0	0	0	0	0	0
Bob Milacki – P (7th)	0	0	0	0	0	0	0	0	0
Mickey Hatcher – PH (9th)	1	0	1	1	0	0	0	0	0

ERR: Kinsler, Denny
LOB: 4

PITCHING:

AL Rookies of the Year	IP	R	ER	H	HR	K	BB
Gary Peters	2	4	4	8	0	1	0
Mark Fidrych (L)	7	2	2	7	1	3	0

AZ All-Time Team	IP	R	ER	H	HR	K	BB
John Denny	6	3	0	7	1	5	0
Alex Kellner	1/3	2	2	2	0	0	0
Bob Milacki (W)	2 2/3	0	0	3	0	1	0

	1	2	3	4	5	6	7	8	9	R	H	E
AL Rookies of the Year	2	1	0	0	0	0	2	0	0	5	12	1
AZ All-Time Team	3	0	1	1	0	0	0	0	1	6	14	2

Arizona's All-Time Team now stands at 7-1, but as you can see, the competition is getting tougher. So what can we do to challenge the greats of the Grand Canyon State even more? How about have them battle a team made up of National League MVPs?

ROSTER
(Team/Year{s} Award Won)

Pitchers:
Bob Gibson *(STL/1968)*
Dazzy Vance *(BRO/1924)*
Bucky Walters *(CIN/1939)*
Mort Cooper *(STL/1942)*
Don Newcombe *(BRO/1956)*
Sandy Koufax *(LA/1963)*
Clayton Kershaw *(LA/2014)*
Carl Hubbell *(NY/1933 & 1936)*
Dizzy Dean *(STL/1934)*
Jim Konstanty *(PHL/1950)*

Catchers
Roy Campanella *(BRO/1951, 1953 & 1955)*
Johnny Bench *(CIN/1970 & 1972)*

Infielders:
Albert Pujols *(STL/2005, 2008 & 2009)*
Rogers Hornsby *(STL & CHI/1925 & 1929)*
Jimmy Rollins *(PHL/2007)*
Mike Schmidt *(PHL/1980, 1981 & 1986)*
Joe Morgan *(CIN/1975 & 1976)*
Ernie Banks *(CHI/1958 & 1959)*
Terry Pendleton *(ATL/1991)*

Outfielders:
Stan Musial *(STL/1943, 1946 & 1948)*
Willie McGee *(STL/1985)*
Joe Medwick *(STL/1937)*
Dale Murphy *(ATL/1982 & 1983)*
Dave Parker *(PIT/1978)*
Andrew McCutchen *(PIT/2013)*

Starting with the first batter, it appeared this would be a long day on the mound for Arizona's Gary Gentry.

Willie McGee began the game with a triple. That was followed by an RBI double by another Cardinal MVP, Joe Medwick. Two batters into the game, the NL MVPs were up 1-0.

Gentry fanned Rogers Hornsby for the first out. Up to the plate came three-time MVP Mike Schmidt. With a sharp crack of the bat, he sent the ball soaring to deep center field. Billy Hatcher gave chase, but pulled up and watched it fall into the seats for a two-run bomb.

Albert Pujols followed with a single, and it appeared the rout was on. Gentry, though, gutted through the inning, striking out Stan Musial and getting Roy Campanella to pop out to short. But the NL MVPs led 3-0.

Arizona responded quickly. Hatcher led off the bottom of the first with a single, then stole second. Bob Gibson struck out Ian Kinsler, then faced Bob Horner. The third baseman clubbed the ball to center. McGee watched it hit the wall above the center field camera well for a two-run homer. Arizona cut the MVPs's lead to one.

Paul Konerko singled, but was thrown out at second when Tim Salmon hit into a fielder's choice. Andre Ethier struck out to end the inning with Arizona down 3-2.

Gentry returned to the hill in the top of the second, looking to keep the game close. First up was Jimmy Rollins. The 2007 MVP from the Phillies lined the ball over the right field fence to give the NL MVPs a 4-2 advantage. After Gibson flew out to right, McGee singled and stole second. The MVPs were in a perfect position to bring home another run with Medwick at bat. A key member of the Cardinals "Gashouse Gang" of the 1930s, he not only won the MVP in 1937, but the Triple Crown with a .374 average, 31 home runs and 154 RBIs.

Medwick hit a sharp grounder to Kinsler. McGee held at second as "Ducky" was thrown out at first. Two down, but another Triple Crown winner stepped into the batter's box. Rogers Hornsby, who batted .403 with 39 homers and 143 RBIs in 1925.

He popped out to short to end the inning.

Gibson gave Arizona no chance to respond in the bottom of the second, as he struck out the side. The third inning was relatively quiet for both sides. In the top of the fourth, Rollins led off with a triple. Next came Gibson, who grounded deep in the hole at short. Rollins took off from third as J.J. Hardy came up with the ball and fired it home. Tom Pagnozzi caught it, brought down his glove and tagged out the sliding Rollins. Gentry struck out McGee and Medwick to close out the inning.

After Gibson set down Arizona 1-2-3 in the bottom of the fourth, the NL MVPs started off the top of the fifth with back-to-back singles by Hornsby and Schmidt. Next came Pujols, who had a combined 368 RBIs in his three MVP seasons.

He grounded to Hardy, who stepped on second for one, then threw to first for the double play. Hornsby advanced safely to third with Musial coming to bat. "The Man" walked, putting runners at the corners with two outs for Campanella. He grounded to Kinsler, who threw to Hardy covering second for the final out.

The bottom of the fifth started with Pagnozzi grounding out to short. Up came Gentry, whom most probably saw as an easy out for Gibson. But the career .095 hitter dumped the ball into the left-center field gap for a base hit. Hatcher followed with a sacrifice bunt, moving Gentry to second. Kinsler then lined the ball into center for a base hit. Gentry raced around third and crossed the plate. Horner flew out to center to end the inning, but Arizona had closed to within one of the NL MVPs, 4-3.

Gentry and Gibson got through their portions of the sixth inning with little trouble. In the seventh, Alex Kellner took over on the mound for Arizona. He gave up back-to-back singles to Hornsby and Schmidt. Pujols came to the plate with runners at the corners and nobody out.

The MVPs first baseman took a huge hack. The ball sailed high over left field. Ethier only took a few steps before watching it go into the patio of TGI Friday's for a three-run homer.

Kellner got the next three batters out, but the NL MVPs upped their lead to 7-3.

Gibson retired the side in order in the seventh. That was his last inning on the mound as Joe Morgan pinch hit for him to lead off the eighth. New Arizona pitcher Lerrin LaGrow worked a 1-1 count on the two-time Most Valuable Player before he drove the ball into the right field stands for the MVPs' fourth home run of the day. After McGee grounded out and pinch hitter Dale Murphy popped out, Hornsby and Schmidt both singled, and the MVPs had another shot of putting this game out of reach with Pujols up.

He popped out to short to end the inning with the MVPs on top 8-3.

Kinsler led off the bottom of the eighth with a single off new pitcher Sandy Koufax. The Dodger lefty then set down the next three batters.

Arizona brought in another new pitcher in the ninth, closer Mike MacDougal. He gave up a ground rule double to pinch hitter Dave Parker to start the inning. After Campanella flew out to right, Rollins hit a double, driving in Parker to make the score 9-3. Pinch hitter Terry Pendleton popped out to second and McGee flew out to center to end the inning.

In the bottom of the ninth, the MVPs brought in Clayton Kershaw to pitch. He walked Ethier and gave up a single to Hardy. Arizona was still in the game with Pagnozzi's replacement, Terry Kennedy, at bat. He grounded out to second, but now Arizona had runners on second and third with Shea Hillenbrand pinch-hitting for MacDougal. He hit a grounder toward left-centerfield. New shortstop Ernie Banks ranged for it and came up throwing.

The ball sailed over the head of first baseman Johnny Bench. Both Ethier and Hardy scored while Hillenbrand went to second. Arizona was now down by four runs and still had a chance.

The next batter was Hatcher, who grounded out to third. It all came down to Kinsler, who was 2-4 with an RBI on the day.

Kershaw got him swinging for strike three, and the NL MVPs got the win 9-5.

NL MVPS	AB	R	H	2B	3B	HR	RBI	K	BB
Willie McGee – CF	6	1	2	0	1	0	0	1	0
Andrew McCutchen – CF (9th)	0	0	0	0	0	0	0	0	0
Joe Medwick – RF	4	1	1	1	0	0	1	1	0
Dale Murphy – PH/RF (8th)	1	0	0	0	0	0	0	0	0
Rogers Hornsby – 2B	5	1	3	0	0	0	0	1	0
Mike Schmidt – 3B	5	2	5	0	0	1	2	0	0
Albert Pujols – 1B	4	1	2	0	0	1	3	0	0
Johnny Bench – PH/1B (8th)	1	0	0	0	0	0	0	0	0
Stan Musial – LF	3	0	0	0	0	0	0	1	1
Dave Parker – PH/LF (9th)	1	1	1	1	0	0	0	0	0
Roy Campanella – C	5	0	0	0	0	0	0	0	0
Jimmy Rollins – SS	5	1	3	1	1	1	2	0	0
Ernie Banks – SS (9th)	0	0	0	0	0	0	0	0	0
Bob Gibson – P	3	0	1	0	0	0	0	0	0
Joe Morgan – PH (8th)	1	1	1	0	0	1	1	0	0
Sandy Koufax – P (8th)	0	0	0	0	0	0	0	0	0
Terry Pendleton – PH (9th)	1	0	0	0	0	0	0	0	0
Clayton Kershaw – P (9th)	0	0	0	0	0	0	0	0	0

SB: McGee
ERR: Hornsby, Banks
LOB: 8

AZ All-Time Team	AB	R	H	2B	3B	HR	RBI	K	BB
Billy Hatcher – CF	4	1	1	0	0	0	0	0	0
Ian Kinsler – 2B	5	0	2	0	0	0	1	2	0
Bob Horner – 3B	4	1	1	0	0	1	2	0	0
Paul Konerko – 1B	4	0	1	0	0	0	0	1	0
Tim Salmon – RF	4	0	1	0	0	0	0	1	0
Andre Ethier – LF	3	1	0	0	0	0	0	2	1
J.J. Hardy – SS	4	1	1	0	0	0	0	2	0
Tom Pagnozzi – C	2	0	0	0	0	0	0	1	0
Terry Kennedy – PH/C (7th)	2	0	0	0	0	0	0	0	0
Gary Gentry – P	2	1	1	0	0	0	0	1	0
Alex Kellner – P (7th)	0	0	0	0	0	0	0	0	0
Hank Leiber – PH (7th)	1	0	0	0	0	0	0	1	0
Lerrin LaGrow – P (8th)	0	0	0	0	0	0	0	0	0
Mike MacDougal – P (9th)	0	0	0	0	0	0	0	0	0
Shea Hillenbrand – PH (9th)	1	0	0	0	0	0	0	0	0

SB: B. Hatcher
SAC: B. Hatcher
LOB: 5

PITCHING:

NL MVPs	IP	R	ER	H	HR	K	BB
Bob Gibson (W)	7	3	3	6	1	9	0
Sandy Koufax	1	0	0	1	0	1	0
Clayton Kershaw	1	2	0	1	0	1	1

AZ All-Time Team	IP	R	ER	H	HR	K	BB
Gary Gentry (L)	6	4	4	11	2	3	1
Alex Kellner	1	3	3	3	1	0	0
Lerrin LaGrow	1	1	1	3	1	0	0
Mike MacDougal	1	1	1	2	0	0	0

	1	2	3	4	5	6	7	8	9	R	H	E
NL MVPs	3	1	0	0	0	0	3	1	1	9	19	2
AZ All-Time Team	2	0	0	0	1	0	0	0	2	5	8	0

The NL MVPs certainly proved a tough opponent, but for the final game for Arizona's All-Time Team, they will face the ultimate challenge. Descending upon Chase Field is a collection of the greatest players who ever stepped onto the diamond. It's Arizona versus a roster made up of Hall of Famers.

ROSTER

Pitchers:
Cy Young
Eddie Plank
Bob Feller
Nolan Ryan
Warren Spahn
Steve Carlton
Early Wynn
Rollie Fingers
Bruce Sutter
Dennis Eckersley

Catchers:
Ernie Lombardi
Mickey Cochrane

Infielders:
Jimmie Foxx
Jackie Robinson
Rabbit Maranville
Brooks Robinson
Harmon Killebrew
Robin Yount
Nap Lajoie

Outfielders:
Rickey Henderson
Ty Cobb
Babe Ruth
Tony Gwynn
Carl Yastrzemski
Hack Wilson

Arizona's All-Time Team had a tall order for this game. The batters had to face baseball's winningest pitcher, the man with the award named after him.

That's right. None other than Cy Young.

It wouldn't be any easier for Arizona starter Gil Heredia. He got the call against a starting line-up featuring a member of the 4,000 hit club (Ty Cobb), the greatest base stealer in history (Rickey Henderson) and one of baseball's greatest home run hitters (Babe Ruth).

Cobb led off the game with a base hit. The man who had 897 career steals surprised no one when he took off for second.

But Tom Pagnozzi showed that no one is immune to his arm behind the plate. He gunned down "The Georgia Peach" for out number one. Henderson popped out to the catcher and Ruth grounded out to second. Three up, three down. Heredia survived his first inning against the Hall of Famers.

Young's first inning went smoothly, the only hiccup a two-out single by Bob Horner. After one inning, the score between these two historic teams was 0-0.

Heredia began the second inning by striking out Jimmie Foxx. Next came the Robinsons, Brooks and Jackie. The former singled and the latter doubled, giving the HOFers runners on second and third with one out. That brought Ernie Lombardi to the plate. He hit a fly to left field. Ethier gave chase, pulled up and made the catch. Brooks Robinson trotted home to put the Hall on top 1-0.

Next was Rabbit Maranville. Heredia ran the count on him to 2-2 when the long-time Boston Braves shortstop laced the ball into left field. Jackie Robinson flew around third and reached home safely. Young popped out to third to end the inning, but the Hall of Famers led 2-0.

The bottom of the second featured a single by Andre Ethier and three flyouts, all to Cobb in center field. Two innings were in the books, with the score still 2-0 Hall.

The top of the third was, in the words of Hall of Famer Yogi Berra, "Deja 'vu all over again." Cobb led off with a single, tried to steal second and was gunned down by Pagnozzi. Henderson then flied out to Ethier in left for out number two. Heredia just had to deal with Ruth to get out of the inning clean.

The Bambino singled. So did the next batter, Foxx. Now it was Brooks Robinson's turn. He drove the ball to left-centerfield. Ethier and Billy Hatcher ran after it.

The ball landed two rows back for a three-run homer by the Oriole great.

Jackie Robinson's groundout to short ended the inning, but the Hall of Famers increased their lead to 5-0.

The bottom of the third started with a pop out to short by Heredia. Hatcher then grounded out to third. Up came Ian Kinsler, who grounded to second.

The ball skipped off Jackie Robinson's glove. He scrambled to pick it up, but was too late to get Kinsler. Next came Horner, who singled to left, advancing Kinsler to third. With runners at the corners and the ever dangerous Paul Konerko up, Arizona had their most serious threat of the day against Young.

The first baseman hit a chopper toward third. Brooks Robinson fielded it cleanly and threw across the field to get Konerko for the third out.

Lombardi led off the top of the fourth for the Hall with a single. Maranville walked, putting runners at first and second with nobody out. Next came Young, a career .210 hitter. He hit a liner toward center. Hatcher raced over and reached out for it.

The ball dropped and rolled to the wall. Lombardi scored. Maranville scored. Young stood on second, helping his own cause with a two-run double.

That would be it for Heredia. He was taken out in favor of Bob Milacki, who retired the first three batters he faced to end the inning, though the Hall had a 7-0 advantage over Arizona.

Young had an easy bottom of the fourth, the only blemish a single by J.J. Hardy. Milacki returned to the hill in the top of the fifth and set down Foxx, Brooks Robinson and Jackie Robinson in order. The Lake Havasu alum also led off the bottom of the inning, but flied out to center. Hatcher followed with a sharp line drive toward left that wound up in the glove of Brooks Robinson. With two down, Kinsler came to the plate. He singled to left. So did the next batter, Horner, his third hit of the day. That brought up Konerko. Young got behind 2-1 and went fastball away.

The Chaparral High grad crushed the ball into the right field seats.

Tim Salmon struck out, but Arizona had finally gotten to Young and cut the Hall's lead to 7-3.

The first batter Milacki faced in the top of the sixth, Ernie Lombardi, singled to left, then made it to second on Maranville's groundout. Young grounded out to third, leaving it up to Cobb to try and extend the Hall's lead. He smoked the ball to center. Hatcher caught it on the bounce and hurled it to the infield as Lombardi rounded third and charged home. The ball skipped past the mound and into Pagnozzi's glove. He swung around to make the tag on the sliding Lombardi.

Out!

Arizona also had a leadoff single to start their half of the sixth, courtesy of Ethier. The next batter was Hardy, who walked. Two on and none out for Pagnozzi. Young worked the count to 1-2, then went to the curve.

Pagnozzi ripped the ball to right field. Ruth ran to the warning track and leaped for it . . .

Gone! The man with 44 home runs in his twelve-year MLB career belted a three-run homer. Arizona now trailed by one run, 7-6.

After striking out Milacki, Young was relieved by Steve Carlton. The four-time Cy Young winner got Hatcher to fly out and Kinsler to pop out to bring the inning to a close.

Tony Gwynn came to the plate to start the top of the seventh, pinch-hitting for Rickey Henderson. He walked, then sprinted for second base. Unlike with Cobb, Pagnozzi could not get Gwynn in time.

After Ruth popped out to the catcher, Foxx came up. He lined the ball to the gap in left-center. Gwynn hustled around third and scored, giving the Hall a little breathing room. Milacki retired both Robinsons to end the inning, but the HOFers increased their lead to 8-6.

Horner led off the bottom of the seventh with his fourth single of the day. He didn't stay on the basepaths long as Konerko grounded into a double play. The inning ended on a Salmon flyout to left.

The Hall got off to a good start against Arizona's new pitcher, Jeremy Affeldt, as Lombardi singled off him. However, the catcher was erased on a 5-4 fielder's choice off the bat of pinch-hitter Robin Yount. Affeldt struck out Carlton and Cobb to close out the inning.

Arizona went in order in the bottom of the eighth. The Hall did likewise in the top of the ninth. Arizona was down to its last at-bat, facing one of the greatest closers, Dennis Eckersley.

First came George Grantham, pinch-hitting for Affeldt. He hit a bouncer to second, fielded by Jackie Robinson's replacement, Nap Lajoie, who threw to first for out number one.

Next it was Hatcher, who grounded to third for the second out.

It all came down to Kinsler to keep Arizona alive.

Three pitches, three strikes, and it was over. The Hall defeated Arizona 8-6.

Hall of Famers	AB	R	H	2B	3B	HR	RBI	K	BB
Ty Cobb – CF	5	0	3	0	0	0	0	2	0
Rickey Henderson – LF	3	0	0	0	0	0	0	0	0
Tony Gwynn – PH/LF (7th)	1	1	0	0	0	0	0	0	1
Babe Ruth – RF	5	1	1	0	0	0	0	0	0
Jimmie Foxx – 1B	3	1	2	0	0	0	1	1	0
Carl Yastrzemski – 1B (8th)	1	0	0	0	0	0	0	1	0
Brooks Robinson – 3B	4	1	2	0	0	1	3	0	0
Jackie Robinson – 2B	4	1	1	0	0	0	0	0	0
Nap Lajoie – 2B (9th)	0	0	0	0	0	0	0	0	0
Ernie Lombardi – C	3	1	3	0	0	0	1	0	0
Rabbit Maranville – SS	3	1	1	0	0	0	1	0	0
Robin Yount – PH/SS (8th)	1	0	0	0	0	0	0	0	0
Cy Young – P	2	0	1	1	0	0	2	0	0
Steve Carlton – P (6th)	2	0	0	0	0	0	0	1	0
Dennis Eckersley – P (9th)	0	0	0	0	0	0	0	0	0

SB: Gwynn
CS: Cobb (2)
SAC FLY: Lombardi
ERR: J. Robinson
LOB: 4

AZ All-Time Team	AB	R	H	2B	3B	HR	RBI	K	BB
Billy Hatcher – CF	5	0	0	0	0	0	0	0	0
Ian Kinsler – 2B	5	1	1	0	0	0	0	1	0
Bob Horner – 3B	4	1	4	0	0	0	0	0	0
Paul Konerko – 1B	4	1	1	0	0	1	3	0	0
Tim Salmon – RF	4	0	0	0	0	0	0	1	0
Andre Ethier – LF	4	1	2	0	0	0	0	0	0
J.J. Hardy – SS	3	1	1	0	0	0	0	0	1
Tom Pagnozzi – C	4	1	1	0	0	1	3	0	0
Gil Heredia – P	1	0	0	0	0	0	0	0	0
Bob Milacki – P (4th)	2	0	0	0	0	0	0	1	0
Jeremy Affeldt – P (8th)	0	0	0	0	0	0	0	0	0
George Grantham – PH (9th)	1	0	0	0	0	0	0	0	0

LOB: 4

PITCHING:

Hall of Famers	IP	R	ER	H	HR	K	BB
Cy Young (W)	5 1/3	6	6	9	2	2	1
Steve Carlton	2 2/3	0	0	1	0	0	0
Dennis Eckersley (SV)	1	0	0	0	0	1	0

AZ All-Time Team	IP	R	ER	H	HR	K	BB
Gil Heredia (L)	3	7	7	10	1	0	1
Bob Milacki	4	1	1	3	0	1	1
Jeremy Affeldt	2	0	0	1	0	3	0

	1	2	3	4	5	6	7	8	9	R	H	E
HOF	0	2	3	2	0	0	1	0	0	8	14	1
AZ All-Time Team	0	0	0	0	3	3	0	0	0	6	10	0

So in ten games, Arizona's All-Time Team ended up 7-3, and in two of those games, it took rosters consisting of some of baseball's greatest players to beat them. Granted, these were simulated games played by using mathematical formulas and dice rolls, but it demonstrated one thing. The state of Arizona has produced some incredibly talented players over the past one hundred years. With so many gifted young men on the fields of Phoenix and Tucson, Prescott and Flagstaff, Yuma and Page, and every other city and town in-between, there is no doubt that more players will represent the Grand Canyon State well over the next one hundred years.

Praise for John J. Rust's sci-fi thriller SEA RAPTOR

"The suspense was excellent. Mr. Rust knows how to use twists in the story to keep the excitement high. A recommended read from me!"
Brenda Whiteside, author of the "Love and Murder" series.

"This is a fast-paced thriller with lots of action, high tension, and a romantic interest. It's a 'man's book', with accompanying 'language', but I enjoyed it. Rust is a good writer and his stories do not disappoint."
Heidi Thomas, author of "Cowgirl Up: A History of Rodeo Women."

Also from John J. Rust

THE BEST PHILLIES TEAM EVER
Mike Schmidt, Richie Ashburn and Chase Utley. They are some of the greatest players to ever suit up for the Philadelphia Phillies. But are they good enough to make the Best Phillies Team Ever? Find out which 25 Phillies earn their spots in the starting lineup, the starting rotation, the bullpen, and on the bench.

SEA RAPTOR
From terrorist hunter to monster hunter. Ex-Army Ranger Jack Rastun joins the Foundation for Undocumented Biological Investigation as they try to stop a sea monster's deadly rampage along the Jersey Shore. But the beast isn't the only threat. A group of murderous animal smugglers also want it. Rastun must utilize every skill learned from years of fighting, otherwise, his first mission for the FUBI could be his last.

23740143R00090

Made in the USA
San Bernardino, CA
28 August 2015